THE
HISTORY OF
PUERTO RICO

ADVISORY BOARD

THE
HISTORY OF
PUERTO RICO

Lisa Pierce Flores

The Greenwood Histories of the Modern Nations
Frank W. Thackeray and John E. Findling, Series Editors

GREENWOOD PRESS
An Imprint of ABC-CLIO, LLC

A B C ⬯ C L I O

Santa Barbara, California • Denver, Colorado • Oxford, England

Library of Congress Cataloging-in-Publication Data

Pierce Flores, Lisa.
  The history of Puerto Rico / by Lisa Pierce Flores.
    p. cm. — (Greenwood histories of the modern nations)
  Includes bibliographical references and index.
  ISBN 978-0-313-35418-2 (hard copy : acid-free paper) — ISBN 978-0-313-35419-9
(ebook) 1. Puerto Rico—History. 2. Puerto Ricans—United States—History. I. Title.
  F1971.P55   2010
  972.95—dc22   2009035279

ISBN: 978-0-313-35418-2
EISBN: 978-0-313-35419-9

14 13 12 11 10   1 2 3 4 5

This book is also available on the World Wide Web as an eBook.
Visit www.abc-clio.com for details.

Praeger
An Imprint of ABC-CLIO, LLC

ABC-CLIO, LLC
130 Cremona Drive, P.O. Box 1911
Santa Barbara, California 93116-1911

This book is printed on acid-free paper (∞)

Manufactured in the United States of America

Contents

An unnumbered photo essay follows page 94.

Series Foreword

The Greenwood Histories of the Modern Nations series is intended to provide students and interested laypeople with up-to-date, concise, and analytical histories of many of the nations of the contemporary world. Not since the 1960s has there been a systematic attempt to publish a series of national histories, and as series advisors, we believe that this series will prove to be a valuable contribution to our understanding of other countries in our increasingly interdependent world.

Some 40 years ago, at the end of the 1960s, the Cold War was an accepted reality of global politics. The process of decolonization was still in progress, the idea of a unified Europe with a single currency was unheard of, the United States was mired in a war in Vietnam, and the economic boom in Asia was still years in the future. Richard Nixon was president of the United States, Mao Tse-tung (not yet Mao Zedong) ruled China, Leonid Brezhnev guided the Soviet Union, and Harold Wilson was prime minister of the United Kingdom. Authoritarian dictators still controlled most of Latin America, the Middle East was reeling in the wake of the Six-Day War, and Shah Mohammad Reza Pahlavi was at the height of his power in Iran.

Since then, the Cold War has ended, the Soviet Union has vanished, leaving 15 independent republics in its wake, the advent of the computer age has radically transformed global communications, the rising demand for oil makes the Middle East still a dangerous flashpoint, and the rise of new economic powers like the People's Republic of China and India threatens to bring about a new world order. All of these developments have had a dramatic impact on the recent history of every nation of the world.

For this series, which was launched in 1998, we first selected nations whose political, economic, and socio-cultural affairs marked them as among the most important of our time. For each nation, we found an author who was recognized as a specialist in the history of that nation. These authors worked cooperatively with us and with Greenwood Press to produce volumes that reflected current research on their nations and that are interesting and informative to their readers. In the first decade of the series, more than 40 volumes were published, and as of 2008, some are moving into second editions.

The success of the series has encouraged us to broaden our scope to include additional nations, whose histories have had significant effects on their regions, if not on the entire world. In addition, geopolitical changes have elevated other nations into positions of greater importance in world affairs and, so, we have chosen to include them in this series as well. The importance of a series such as this cannot be underestimated. As a super-power whose influence is felt all over the world, the United States can claim a "special" relationship with almost every other nation. Yet many Americans know very little about the histories of nations with which the United States relates. How did they get to be the way they are? What kind of political systems have evolved there? What kind of influence do they have on their own regions? What are the dominant political, religious, and cultural forces that move their leaders? These and many other questions are answered in the volumes of this series.

The authors who contribute to this series write comprehensive histories of their nations, dating back, in some instances, to prehistoric times. Each of them, however, has devoted a significant portion of their book to events of the past 40 years because the modern era has contributed the most to con-temporary issues that have an impact on U.S. policy. Authors make every effort to be as up-to-date as possible so that readers can benefit from discus-sion and analysis of recent events.

In addition to the historical narrative, each volume contains an introduc-tory chapter giving an overview of that country's geography, political insti-tutions, economic structure, and cultural attributes. This is meant to give readers a snapshot of the nation as it exists in the contemporary world. Each history also includes supplementary information following the narra-tive, which may include a timeline that represents a succinct chronology of the nation's historical evolution, biographical sketches of the nation's most important historical figures, and a glossary of important terms or concepts that are usually expressed in a foreign language. Finally, each author prepares a comprehensive bibliography for readers who wish to pursue the subject further.

Readers of these volumes will find them fascinating and well written. More importantly, they will come away with a better understanding of the contemporary world and the nations that comprise it. As series advisors, we hope that this series will contribute to a heightened sense of global understanding as we move through the early years of the twenty-first century.

Frank W. Thackeray and John E. Findling
Indiana University Southeast

Preface

As I was working on this project I was asked many times why a book on Puerto Rico would be included in a series called *The Greenwood Histories of Modern Nations*. "Puerto Rico is not a nation," I was told triumphantly time and again (though never by Puerto Ricans). "It's part of the United States." Another popular response was: "What exactly is the deal with Puerto Rico?" Many non-Puerto Ricans I spoke with were not sure if Puerto Rico was part of the United States or not, whether Puerto Ricans living in the United States were immigrants, and if not, my interlocutors wanted to know, why not.

When I told Puerto Rican family and friends about my project, responses were too varied to include here; however, I noticed that no one ever brought up the "Puerto Rico isn't a nation" argument. Puerto Ricans living on and off the island—even if our ties to the island are several generations distant—seem to have an intrinsic perception of Puerto Rico as a nation, even if it is not currently a nation-state. A history on the geographic, cultural entity that is the ancestral home of nearly 8 million people should and must be included in a series of books on modern nations. When I told Puerto Ricans about my project, I received nods of approval, offers of help, and tireless disquisitions on various aspects of Borinquen (Puerto Rican) culture and politics, particularly on the status issue.

WHAT'S THE DEAL WITH PUERTO RICO?

According to the Puerto Rican government, Puerto Rico is currently a commonwealth or freely associated state of the United States. According to the U.S. government, Puerto Rico is an unincorporated territory of the United States. It is "unincorporated" because it is not on a path toward statehood. If it were on the path toward statehood it would be called an "incorporated" territory. It is a "territory" because it has a close association with the United States that, according to U.S. legal definitions, "freely associated states," such as Micronesia, do not enjoy, including interest-free social welfare subsidies. Puerto Rico's unique relationship with the United States means that its citizens carry U.S. passports, vote in presidential primaries (though not elections), and can be drafted into the military. So how, one might ask, can Puerto Rico be considered a nation?

Although a nation-state has been defined as a sovereign political entity with defined boundaries, a nation can be defined as a community of people who believe they have shared traits, a common heritage, and collective goals, such as a right to self-determination. Using this definition, Puerto Rico can and should be thought of as a nation.

A nation-state is a fairly recent concept. In fact, according to many historians and political scientists, the concept dates no further back than the late nineteenth century. In Chapter 3 of this book I trace the complicated route by which the many traditional historic and cultural entities that made up the nations of the Iberian Peninsula organized themselves into what

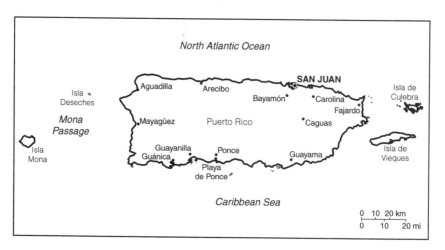

Puerto Rico. [Cartography by Bookcomp, Inc.]

we today think of as the nation-state of Spain. I do this because it has important implications for the ethnic, economic, and cultural evolution of the Puerto Rican landscape and the Puerto Rican people during the Spanish colonial period, but the narrative in that chapter also serves as an example of how European nations evolved into the complex political entities we post-Modernists think of as nation-states.

Perhaps more important than political and historical definitions are the ways people choose to identify and define themselves. Puerto Ricans living on the island and in the United States often refer to Puerto Rico—as opposed to the Puerto Rican Diaspora—as *el país* or *la patria*, meaning the country, the nation, the homeland. The simplest answer to the question of how a landmass that is not recognized as a sovereign political entity by the rest of the world can be called a nation is because its people believe that it is one.

NOTES ON THE TEXT

Puerto Rico's political status presents some unique challenges to the writer. Throughout the text I have tended to use terms like "the island" or "on the island" to refer to activities that took place on the landmass of Puerto Rico (though it consists of more than one island). U.S. courts have ruled that Puerto Rico is a territory *of* the United States but *not part* of the United States, a fine distinction that makes it nearly impossible to discuss interactions between island and mainland Puerto Ricans without using cumbersome or even unintentionally politicized language. With no other objective but clarity I have tended to use phrases such as "stateside," "in the States," and "Puerto Ricans living in the United States" to refer to Puerto Rican migrants living in the 50 United States. Of course, it could be argued that this terminology makes no sense if you believe, as many people do, that Puerto Rico is part of the United States. Even some U.S. court opinions differ on this matter. I have chosen to use the term "migrant" to describe Puerto Ricans living in the 50 United States because U.S. citizens are not and cannot by definition be immigrants. I have chosen to use phrases like "on the island" and "in the States" because these are phrases used by Puerto Ricans to describe and differentiate themselves.

I have chosen to concentrate on the history of Puerto Ricans living on the island and have not attempted to incorporate the long history of Puerto Ricans living in the United States. I have made this choice because it would have been too difficult to tackle the complexity of the sometimes parallel and often intersecting histories of Puerto Ricans living on the island and the Puerto Rican Diaspora in the United States (and elsewhere) within the scope of this book. Luckily for students interested in the history of Puerto Ricans in the

United States, this rich area of study includes many excellent sources that are accessible for students and general readers. I have included a selection of them in the Bibliographic Essay. I concede that the relationship between the two communities is more intricate and interconnected than I have been able to explore in any detail here. Indeed, I have only mentioned the Puerto Rican Diaspora in short segments when their activities had a direct effect on events transpiring on the island. In the future, I look forward to sources that will take a parallel view of the histories of both communities—or perhaps one can argue that it is, in some respects, a single community.

I have tried to supply English translations for Spanish phrases throughout the text and in the Glossary. When referring to historical figures by their last names I have used both the father's surname, which usually comes after a person's first name in Spanish, and their mother's surname, which typically appears last, after the father's surname. That is why two names are typically given to refer to persons in the text. For example, I have used "Albizu Campos," or occasionally "Albizu," to refer to Pedro Albizu Campos.

Another choice I have made is to include a chapter on indigenous people, rather than the cursory mention that is characteristic of most general histories of the island written in English. I have also devoted much of the text to pre-twentieth century history, which may seem unusual given the focus of this series. I have done this because many Puerto Rican students in the United States do not have easy access to this information and because studies have shown that a growing number of Latino students often ask for and crave such information. Puerto Rico's long history is barely mentioned in most U.S. textbooks, despite the unique relationship that Puerto Rico shares with the U.S. government. The Caribbean is barely mentioned in many American History textbooks even though Christopher Columbus' earliest explorations led him there and despite the fact that the narrative of European colonization and indigenous interaction for the next 400 years was largely determined by the events that occurred in the Dominican Republic, Puerto Rico, and their Caribbean neighbors at the turn of the sixteenth century.

As I began researching this text I was completing work on a larger project for Greenwood/ABC-CLIO called *The American Mosaic,* a set of Web sites and blogs exploring the American multiethnic experience. Working simultaneously on the American Indian component of this larger project and the preliminary research for this volume I was struck by how events that took place more than 500 years ago in Puerto Rico and the Dominican Republic had shaped the discourse of European contact with the indigenous peoples of North America that was to take place almost 100 years later. Here was the origin of the inaccurate term "Indian" and the offensive "red man," the arbitrarily assigned duality between the "good Indian" and the "bad Indian," and the origin of the "disappearing" or "extinct" Indian. In the words of archeologist and historian Kathleen Deagan:

> The Taínos were the first group of indigenous American men and women to encounter and live with Europeans. . . . The critical first decades of interaction between Taínos and Spaniards had a profound influence on subsequent European beliefs about, understanding of, and policy toward America and its inhabitants.[1]

Yet, even the indigenous scholarship I was working with rarely made more than a cursory connection to the earliest European-Amerindian contact because it was part of Hispanic, and not Anglo-American history. For this and other reasons, I chose to focus part of my history on the Taíno people and the other indigenous peoples of the island. Perhaps the contemporary movement to reclaim this history and incorporate it into Puerto Rican identity is as good a justification as any for its prominence in a history that is part of a series on "Modern Nations."

FAMILY HISTORY

Because I am a journalist and writing teacher, I chose to approach this project as the student I once was, armed with the research skills I had accumulated over the course of 20 years as a reporter and editor. Since I am not a historian, I knew that I could not give a definitive scholarly account of the island. Instead, I have tried to focus on my intended audience—students and general researchers—and to remember my own frustrations as a Puerto Rican growing up in the United States, several generations removed from my family's years on the island, trying to find out whatever I could about who I was.

As a result, I have tried to provide a general history that mentions areas that could easily lead the student to more intensive, detailed study, and I have provided a detailed Bibliographic Essay intended to give students some ideas of how to begin researching those more specific research projects. I have tried to provide a "big picture" of the island's history and I have tried to make that history as accurate and inclusive as possible. The inclusive part was important to me for personal as well as professional reasons. Growing up I knew that my mother's family had never made any secret of their African ancestry, but they also talked about the customs they had inherited from their Taíno-Carib family members, some of whom were not part of the "distant" past. They may not have used words like indigenous or Taíno, but when they talked about a grandparent or great-grandparent from "the interior" that is what they meant.

As a college student, I began researching my heritage and internalized critiques of indigenous ancestral claims that, according to the historians, could not be true because the indigenous population had disappeared shortly after the appearance of the European explorers, though they brought no women with them initially, came in small numbers, and yet somehow proliferated. According to historians, claims of indigenous ancestry must be the result of Puerto Ricans' racist endeavors to erase, or at least mitigate, their African ancestry. This has until recently been the narrative that awaits Puerto Rican students studying their heritage. Looking back, the critique makes no sense. Like most Puerto Ricans I know my own family has always described themselves as "brown" and even those of us who are, like me and my mother, closer to "beige," readily admit to a racial heritage that is "una mezcla," a mixture.

I have tried to include as much information as I could on Afro-Puerto Rican, indigenous, and European and U.S. aspects of the island's history and culture, focusing where appropriate on new research uncovered by archeologists and scholars of indigenous culture, as well as information on slavery and slave revolts uncovered by contemporary Afro-Puerto Rican scholars. Taking their cue from the multicultural studies movement of the late twentieth century, many Puerto Rican scholars have literally uncovered new ground during the past few decades in the form of archeological digs. Others have begun sifting through previously neglected documents on Afro-Puerto Rican history. This research has changed and will continue to change the narrative of Puerto Rican history, creating a more inclusive and more accurate picture of the last 4,000 years.

As my research unfolded, I began to piece together my own family history. Fragments that had never before formed a complete picture began to come together and a clearer image of their life story came into focus. For example, it made sense that my great-grandfather, José Flores, from the tobacco-producing region of San Lorenzo, would open a cigar shop in Manhattan in the 1920s. The tobacco industry's downturn and the passage of the Jones Act made sense of the timing of his migration to the United States. Growing up in San Lorenzo, where he worked as a cigar roller (and semi-professional baseball player) for the local cigar and cigarette factory, provided him with the expertise he needed to open a small shop that sold hand-rolled and imported cigars. My new knowledge of San Lorenzo, the tobacco industry, and the prominence of women within that industry also made sense of a greater and more scandalous mystery from my early childhood—why some of the older women in my family smoked cigars!

ACKNOWLEDGMENTS

My career in journalism and my connection to my Latino heritage—as my struggles to find material about Puerto Rican history and culture during my teenage years attest—would not have been possible had it not been for an internship arranged during my sophomore year of college by my parents, Robert Pierce and Felicity Flores Pierce; my grandfather, the late Thomas Flores; and Venezuelan journalists Rafael Poleo and his daughter (my mother's stepsister) Patricia Poleo. The Poleos generously allowed me to spend the summer of 1988 as the least helpful intern any newsroom has likely ever seen.

My mother is due a second dose of gratitude for her support, both emotional and linguistic, during the course of my research for this book.

My editor, Kaitlin Ciarmiello, has been kind, attentive, and above all, patient. I am indebted to her careful reading and attention to detail. Series Editors Frank Thackery and John Finding also provided useful suggestions. While dividing my time between researching this book and serving as Web editor of *The American Mosaic*, Ilan Stavans, the late Maria Chavez-Hernandez, and all the members of the *Latino American Experience* Advisory Board provided inspiration for me to keep researching and writing, as did my always supportive boss, Kevin Ohe.

Like everything I have done since I first met my husband eighteen years ago, this book is a collaboration—a project I could not have accomplished without his support, encouragement, and feedback. This time it is literally true; his photo of Ponce appears on the cover.

Finally, I dedicate this effort to my grandparents, Josephine and Thomas Flores, and my great-grandparents, José, Félin, Luis, and Mary, all of whom found their way to the New York *colonia*.

Timeline of Historical Events

2000 BCE	First human inhabitants settle in mangroves of Puerto Rico.
500–200 BCE	Saladoid people arrive in Puerto Rico bringing advanced agricultural and pottery skills.
1200 CE	Artistically sophisticated Saladoid people give way to the emergence of the highly politically organized Taíno people, ushering in the Taíno Florescence, a period of artistic, political, and agricultural accomplishment. Puerto Rico was only one of many islands inhabited by the Taíno, whose villages and towns throughout the Greater and Lesser Antilles were connected by trade routes and ruling-class (*nitaínos*) bloodlines.
1450 CE	Taíno begin to experience attacks from Carib people, who capture Taíno women as brides.
September 25, 1493	Italian explorer Christopher Columbus leaves Port of Cadiz in Spain for his Second Voyage to the Americas, on which he will "discover" Puerto Rico.

November 19, 1493	A group of Taíno women and children guide Columbus to the island they call Borinquen, where he probably landed near the port of Aguada or Cabo Rojo. He remains for two days and names the island San Juan Bautista.
August 12, 1508	Juan Ponce de León settles on the island with 42 men, becoming the first governor of San Juan Bautista, the Spanish name for Borinquen (Puerto Rico).
December 1508	Ponce de León establishes the settlement of Caparra, which is later relocated to present-day Old San Juan.
1510–1511	Taíno Uprising (often referred to as the Taíno-Carib Uprising) results in the deaths of as many as 200 Spanish settlers before its eventual defeat by Juan Ponce de León.
1512	Juana I of Castile issues the Laws of the Burgos, which creates guidelines for the treatment of the Taíno by the Spanish colonists. Most of the provisions of the laws are ignored.
January 1517	4,000 slaves from Africa arrive in Puerto Rico, though small numbers of African slaves were brought to the island as early as 1512.
1521	Ponce de León, first governor of Puerto Rico, dies of injuries inflicted by indigenous Calusa people of Florida.
1522	San José Church is built in San Juan. It is the second oldest Christian church in the Americas.
1523	First sugar cane processing plant built.
1530	First census taken by Francisco Manuel de Lando.
1537	Construction begins on La Fortaleza, the building that still serves as the governor's mansion, by some accounts the oldest continuously used government building in the Americas.
April 1539	Construction begins on El Morro fort.
1543	Spain orders the emancipation of Taíno and Carib slaves, though few remain. Some of those freed join previously escaped Taíno-Caribs to set up communities in the interior, where they maintained many of their customs and beliefs away from interference by the Spanish for centuries.

1582	Spain begins to provide colonists on the island (now referred to as Puerto Rico or "the rich port" rather than San Juan Bautista) with the *situado*, a stipend, to help pay for fortifications, public works, and soldiers' salaries.
November 1595	Englishman Sir Frances Drake attacks Puerto Rico and is repelled.
June 1598	George Clifford, Earl of Cumberland, attacks, and portions of the island are briefly under English rule before he is repelled.
1625	Dutch fleet commander Boudewijn Hendriksz lays siege to San Juan before his forces are defeated and he is forced to retreat.
1765	Alejandro de O'Reilly comes to the island to undertake an extensive census, which the Spanish use to determine future policy for developing the island's agricultural and economic potential.
1797	British General Ralph Abercromby attacks Puerto Rico and controls an area just outside San Juan for two weeks before he is defeated and forced to retreat by Spanish forces aided by local volunteer militia.
1811	Ramón Power y Giralt becomes Puerto Rico's first democratically elected representative, charged with communicating the interests of the Puerto Rican people in the Spanish government. In Cadiz, Spain, he is elected vice president of parliament and helps to draft the first Spanish Constitution.
1812	Spanish Constitution ratified in Cadiz, declaring Puerto Rico a Spanish province.
1815	Cédula de Gracias, or Warrant of Opportunity, decreed by Spain, offering land grants and tax breaks to Catholics from other countries willing to relocate to Puerto Rico.
1826	Governor Miguel de la Torre issues the *Reglamento de Esclavos* (Slave Regulations) authorizing slave owners to use brutal methods to prevent slaves from revolting.
1848	Governor Juan Prim issues the *Banda Contra la Raza Africana* (called the Black Code), which strips away protections against the abuse of African slaves and takes away

	the rights of free Afro-Puerto Ricans to legal redress in physical disputes with whites, even if those disputes lead to murder.
1849	Governor Juan de la Pezuela issues the law of *libreta*, or *Reglamento de Jornaleros* (Workers' Regulations), which requires all agricultural workers to carry a passbook to prove that they are employed by a large landowner.
1854	Puerto Rico annexes Vieques.
1855	Cholera epidemic kills 30,000 residents, or about six percent of the total population of more than 492,000.
September 23, 1868	Grito de Lares uprising, 600 revolutionaries capture the government office of Lares and proclaim the Republic of Puerto Rico. Unable to capture any other municipalities, they are chased into the mountains and arrested as traitors.
1873	Slavery abolished by Spanish government; Spain's constitutional monarchy is replaced by a republican form of government.
1876	Spain establishes El Yunque as a reserve.
1890	Luis Muñoz Rivera founds the influential pro-independence newspaper *La Democracia*.
November 15, 1897	Spain ratifies *Carta Autonómica* (Autonomic Charter), which grants Puerto Rico substantial political and administrative autonomy, while still maintaining its affiliation with Spain.
April 12, 1898	Spanish-American War begins.
July 25, 1898	American troops, led by General Nelson Miles, invade Puerto Rico.
August 12, 1898	Treaty of Paris cedes control of Puerto Rico to the United States.
October 18, 1898	General John R. Brooke becomes the first of many U.S. military and civil governors appointed by the U.S. President.
1900	Foraker Act (First Organic Act of Puerto Rico) passed by U.S. Congress establishing a system of government dominated by U.S. officials appointed by the U.S. President and various divisions of the U.S. War Department.
1903	University of Puerto Rico established.

December 5, 1916	Jones Act approved by U.S. Congress establishes a slight increase in governing power for elected Puerto Rican officials in partnership with appointed U.S. officials, but U.S. officials retain the bulk of control. In addition, the Jones Act grants U.S. citizenship to Puerto Ricans.
1930	Pedro Albizu Campos becomes president of the pro-independence Nationalist Party.
1936	Suffrage granted to all women. Educated women had been given the vote in 1932.
February 23, 1936	Police Commissioner Francis E. Riggs is assassinated, setting off a string of arrests of Nationalists (members of the pro-independence party) and violence, leading to the arrest and imprisonment of Pedro Albizu Campos.
March 21, 1937	Shots are fired at a pro-independence march in Ponce killing at least 19 and injuring 100, though some have put the casualty toll much higher. The incident is called the Ponce Massacre and triggers unrest that leads President Franklin Roosevelt to replace the unpopular governor, Blanton Winship.
1940	Luis Muñoz Marín's autonomist Popular Democratic Party (PDP) wins a majority of seats in the legislature. The PDP remains in power for the next three decades.
1941	World War II begins, thousands of Puerto Ricans are assigned to military units on the island and in the United States.
1942	Liberal reformer Rexford Tugwell becomes the last non-Puerto Rican appointed governor. He and Senate President Luis Muñoz Marín form a partnership instituting widespread social and economic changes during the next five years.
1946	Jesús Piñero becomes the first Puerto Rican governor. He is the last governor appointed by a U.S. President.
1947	U.S. Congress approves the Puerto Rican people's right to elect their own governor.
June 1948	Governor Jesús Piñero signs the "Gag Law" (*Ley de la Mordaza*, also known as Law 53), which prohibits any pro-Nationalist rhetoric under the argument that any expression calling for an independent Puerto Rico is sedition encouraging the overthrow of the U.S.

	government. Under the law even displaying the Puerto Rican flag is punishable by fine or up to ten years in prison.
January 2, 1949	Luis Muñoz Marín is sworn in as Puerto Rico's first democratically elected governor.
October 30–November 1, 1950	Nationalist Insurrection of 1950, includes violent uprisings in several municipalities on the island and attempted assassinations of Governor Muñoz Marín in San Juan and President Harry Truman in New York City. Weapons are confiscated from Albizu Campos' car and 140 Nationalists, including Albizu, are arrested.
1951	Puerto Rico's constitution drafted and approved by U.S. Congress, after portions are amended at the insistence of Congressional members.
1952	U.S. Congress and the Puerto Rican people ratify constitution, making Puerto Rico a commonwealth or freely associated state (*Estado Libre Asociado*).
1954	Nationalists fire shots from the visitors' gallery of the U.S. House of Representatives in Washington, D.C., wounding several Congressmen.
1965	Nationalist leader Pedro Albizu Campos dies.
1967	First Plebiscite (referendum) on Puerto Rico's status is held; the majority of voters select commonwealth status over statehood and independence.
1972	National hero and baseball star Roberto Clemente is killed in a plane crash.
April 30, 1980	Luis Muñoz Marín, Puerto Rico's first elected governor, dies.
1989	Hurricane Hugo causes destruction throughout the island.
1993	Commonwealth status reaffirmed in Second Plebiscite.
1998	Island-wide, non-binding referendum held on Puerto Rico's status; most voters select "none of the above" from a slate of options, including independence and continued commonwealth status. Statehood garners the second most votes.

1998–1999	Pro-labor protests held in opposition to the government's policy of selling publicly owned utilities such as telephone service to foreign investors.
1999	Military accident on Vieques kills a civilian guard and injures four other Puerto Ricans, leading to several years of protests demanding that the U.S. military stop conducting military maneuvers and weapons testing on Vieques and/or shut down the island's military base.
2000	Sila M. Calderon becomes the island's first woman governor.
2001	President George W. Bush orders an end to test bombing on Vieques beginning in 2003.
2004	The U.S. military base in Vieques is shut down and the grounds made into a nature preserve by the U.S. government.
2005, 2007	The President's Task Force on Puerto Rico's Status issues reports stating that the current commonwealth status does not in fact constitute the legal definition of a freely associated state and urging periodic plebiscites that would include more detail for voters on the legal boundaries of their status options.
2009	Protests held in opposition to Governor Luis Guillermo Fortuño-Burset's extensive cuts in government jobs in response to the worldwide economic downturn, which hit Puerto Rico's economy especially hard.
May 2009	Puerto Rico's Resident Commissioner Pedro Pierluisi submits the Puerto Rico Democracy Act of 2009 (H.R. 2499) to Congress. The bill calls for a plebiscite that would contain two options for Puerto Rican voters: remaining under the island's present commonwealth status or opting for a follow-up plebiscite with a variety of governance options, ranging from statehood to independence. The pro-statehood party favors the bill, while the pro-commonwealth and pro-independence parties have voiced opposition to it.

1

Puerto Rico and Its People

Nations have been defined any number of ways. For many, a "nation" calls to mind a nation-state, a self-contained, sovereign entity whose political boundaries correspond to ethnic or cultural borders. This type of political entity is a fairly recent concept and was not commonly in existence at the time that Spain colonized Puerto Rico in the early sixteenth century.

In contrast to a nation-state, a nation, as defined in *The American Heritage College Dictionary* (4th ed.), is a "people who share common customs, origins, history, and frequently language; a nationality." By this definition, Puerto Rico is a nation. In addition to its shared customs, culture, and language, Puerto Rico has clearly defined borders, a democratically elected internal government, a unique ethnic heritage and culture, and a history that goes back over 4,000 years. This history's narrative consists of common, recurring themes, not the least of which are a desire for sovereignty and a struggle to maintain and define its culture in opposition to larger, more powerful external cultural and political entities, first Spain and then the United States. This continuity, along with the unrelenting ability of the Puerto Rican people to adapt to outside forces without letting go of their rituals, beliefs, language, and culture, defines Puerto Rico as a nation. Though Puerto Rico's ultimate political future is still uncertain, the determination of its people to insist on their own definitions of *puertorriquenidad* (literally, what it means to be Puerto Rican) will exist as long as the entity that is Puerto Rico exists.

THE LAND

Puerto Rico is the smallest and easternmost of the Greater Antilles, a system of islands in the Caribbean Ocean. The political entity referred to as Puerto Rico consists of three islands—Puerto Rico, Vieques, and Culebra—with a combined area of 13,790 square miles. The main island is 100 miles long and 34 miles across and lies east of the Dominican Republic, across a section of water referred to as the Mona Pass. The two islands are so close that it is believed that the indigenous Taíno people traveled across by canoe daily.

Puerto Rico's climate is tropical, though there is enough variation of seasons to create a distinct growing season, with slightly colder temperatures in the winter and hotter weather in the summer. Temperatures are slightly cooler in the mountainous regions. Hurricanes are frequent. Though Puerto Rico is a small landmass, it contains diverse terrain, including a rain forest, mountain range, fertile coastal plain in the south, and a dry, arid coast in the north.

The history of human habitation on the island has been affected by its relationship to the Gulf Stream, which is created by the joining of two major currents: the South Equatorial Current and the North Equatorial Current. The South Equatorial Current moves west from Africa, then swirls along the upper coast of South America and Central America into the Gulf of Mexico and Florida Straits. The North Equatorial Current travels east across the northern side of the Greater Antilles. These currents join to create the powerful Gulf Stream. What this essentially means for Puerto Rico is that travel to the island is easier south to north, east to west—the directions by which various waves of explorers and invaders have been coming to the island for 4,000 years, ever since there has been human habitation on the island. In addition to the Gulf Stream and its equatorial currents, there is a countercurrent that travels east along the southern side of the island. For this reason, Pre-Contact historians believe that two groups of settlers came to the island: one traveling east from the Yucatan and another north from South America. So, despite the relatively short distance between Florida and Cuba, it is unlikely Amerindians from Florida ever came to the Greater Antilles, which explains why Puerto Rican societies more closely resembled the civilizations of Mesoamerica than those of the American Indians from the region that later became Florida.

The Trade Winds later brought explorers from Europe, especially after Juan Ponce de León discovered how the Gulf Stream facilitated westward journeys to the Caribbean. The Trade Winds affect the climate and topography of Puerto Rico as well. During most of the year the Trade Winds blow in a northeasterly direction, bringing heavy rain to the northern and eastern parts of the island where the mountains of the Sierra de Luquillo range and the lush valleys of the rain forest are found. In contrast, little rain falls on the semiarid southern coast.

El Yunque rain forest (the U.S. Forest Service officially refers to it as the Caribbean National Forest, Luquillo Division) is home to a diverse range of wildlife, including more than 100 species of butterflies, 270 kinds of birds, 16 species of the coquí frog, and 25 species of lizards, including some of the smallest varieties in the world.

Puerto Ricans refer to their island as *"el país,"* or the country. For Puerto Ricans living on the U.S. mainland, La Isla refers to the island of Puerto Rico, but to Puerto Ricans living on the island, La Isla refers to the cities, towns, and rural areas outside of San Juan. Though the majority of present-day Puerto Ricans live in cities, many still retain a romantic image of the *campo,* or country, and of the *jíbaro,* the rural worker. On the island it is not unusual to hear people say that *la isla,* or *el campo,* is where the Puerto Rican heart is.

THE PEOPLE

There are more than 3.9 million people living in Puerto Rico and another 4 million people of Puerto Rican descent living in the United States. Puerto Ricans are U.S. citizens with a complicated governance relationship with the United States explained in the Government section of this chapter. Puerto Rico's relationship with the United States has allowed it to take advantage of social programs and health care services, providing it with one of the region's highest qualities of life, including a high literacy rate, low infant mortality, and life expectancy of 78 for men and 82 for women.

About 75 percent of Puerto Ricans living on the island are Roman Catholic, with a growing number of Protestants. Spanish is the official and primary language, though many people—and nearly all young people— speak English as well. Puerto Ricans living on and off the island are the descendants of Amerindian, African, and European settlers to the island.

The *jíbaro* has long served as a powerful cultural and political symbol for Puerto Ricans, particularly for the independence and autonomist movements. *Jíbaro* literally means farmer, but for the majority urban population, the *jíbaro* is a symbol of the past, a romantic figure who embodies the pride the people feel for the beauty and history of their island. Even among

Puerto Ricans who do not support independence, the *jíbaro* prompts an emotional connection.

Contemporary Puerto Ricans are proud of their cultural past and participate in a number of activities that pay homage to their Spanish, African, and indigenous ancestry. Traditional cultural endeavors include a pride in the Spanish language and literature, including a rich island canon. Poetry is especially revered on the island and many of the country's most important political figures, including twentieth-century leaders like Pedro Albizu Campos and Luis Muñoz Marín, were also published poets. Music, and especially dance, are also important elements of the traditional culture, particularly native forms that combine Spanish and African elements to create uniquely Caribbean means of expression. At the same time, a younger generation of Puerto Ricans has come to see themselves as consumers and creators of a new hybrid culture that encompasses North American–dominated consumer culture and media and processes them through the lens of a bilingual, multiethnic, Caribbean experience unique to Puerto Ricans because of the island's relationship with the United States. This blended cultural and artistic attitude can be heard in Puerto Rican hip hop, seen in Puerto Rican film, and understood through a new wave of Puerto Rican literature that especially gravitates toward memoir.

THE ECONOMY

Puerto Rico is considered a middle-class economy by the World Bank and has one of the healthiest economies and highest standard of living in the Caribbean and Latin American region. Its currency is the U.S. dollar, and it enjoys duty-free access to the U.S. market, as well as some special tax breaks designed to attract foreign investment, an important element in the economy since the 1950s. Once an agricultural center and one of the world's top producers of sugar, coffee, and tobacco, Puerto Rico's economy shifted to manufacturing in the 1950s. By the 1980s, the economy had shifted from textile and other forms of traditional manufacturing to pharmaceutical and small consumer electronic production; however, the island still generates a fair share of export revenue from rum, a sugar-derived product. Tourism is also a source of income. Because the economy is so closely tied to the U.S. market, the economy contracted slightly in 2007 and 2008, mirroring the downturn in the U.S. economy.

THE GOVERNMENT

Since 1952 Puerto Rico has operated as a Commonwealth (called a Freely Associated State or *Estado Libre Asociado* by the internal government) and enjoyed internal self-rule. It is officially referred to as The Commonwealth of Puerto Rico or El Estado Libre Asociado de Puerto Rico. Puerto Ricans elect a governor, an island-wide bicameral legislature, and local municipal leaders, all of whom govern according to a constitution, which was drafted and ratified by island residents, but approved by the U.S. Congress. The three main insular political parties represent three options for the island's status: sustained Commonwealth status, statehood, and independence.

Puerto Ricans are U.S. citizens but field their own Olympic team. They serve in the U.S. military and can be conscripted, but do not have a voting delegation to the U.S. Congress and they do not vote for President. The U.S. Democratic and Republican parties both hold presidential primaries in Puerto Rico. A Resident Commissioner is elected by the voters to represent the interests of the Puerto Rican people to the U.S. government and can speak before the U.S. House of Representatives, but cannot vote.

The island capital is San Juan, as it has been for nearly 500 years. The island has 78 municipalities, each with a locally democratically elected governing apparatus. The legal system consists of municipal courts and a system of appellate and superior courts; however, cases that test jurisdiction between internal and federal government are decided by the U.S. federal court system.

According to certain interpretations of the U.S. Constitution recently endorsed by the *Report by the President's Task Force on Puerto Rico's Status* (2007), Puerto Rico is an unincorporated, organized territory of the United States with Commonwealth status. The importance of incorporation, according to the U.S. Constitution, is that an incorporated territory would be undergoing the official steps necessary to become a state. In addition, if Puerto Rico were actually a freely associated state with the United States, under the definition accepted by the U.S. Constitution, then it would be an independent country and could no longer be provided with some of the social programs and tax benefits it currently enjoys.

Puerto Ricans carry a U.S. passport and if they move to the United States can vote in Congressional and Presidential elections.

Puerto Rico's political situation is unique and complicated and the focus of much of its internal party politics as well as its history.

2

Borinquen: Origins and Encounter (4000 BCE–1500 CE)

Until the late twentieth century, most histories of Puerto Rico began with cursory mentions of the island's pre-colonial era. In some cases, books on the island simply began with the arrival of Columbus in Puerto Rico in 1493. (Traditionally, historians maintained that the island's indigenous inhabitants had quickly disappeared in the first few decades after the arrival of the *conquistadores*, victims of disease, warfare, and brutality.) Furthermore, mid-twentieth-century historians and political scientists argued, the indigenous peoples of the Caribbean had not significantly affected the cultural life of the island from the colonial era to the present. As recently as the late 1990s and early 2000s, many prominent Caribbean and Latin American historians maintained that the ethnic contributions of the Taíno, Carib, and other indigenous groups were insignificant when compared to the European and African genetic inheritance embodied in present-day Puerto Ricans living on the island and in the United States.

Despite this widely held argument, students in Puerto Rico (as well as Puerto Rican students at many U.S. universities) in the 1970s began demanding classes on Pre-Contact Puerto Rico and have continued to demand information on this era ever since. In addition, civic life on the island and in Puerto Rican communities in the United States has often embraced and celebrated the indigenous elements of Puerto Rican identity. This continued interest among everyday Puerto Ricans in the island's pre-colonial past has driven scholarship. At the same time, over the past several decades, archeologists and other historians have been building the case for a strong indigenous influence on the culture of Puerto Rico. It seems appropriate that a contemporary general history of the island should devote at least one chapter to the Pre-Contact history of the island from the perspective of the people who lived there prior to the arrival of Columbus.

PRE-CONTACT PUERTO RICO

The first inhabitants of Puerto Rico left no written history. To understand the cultures of the people who settled the island prior to 1493, historians and scientists have had to piece together fragments of a historical puzzle. These historians and scientists specialize in the study of Pre-Contact America. Pre-Contact refers to the era prior to the arrival of Europeans in the Americas. Other terms for Pre-Contact include Pre-Encounter and Prehistory.

To understand what Puerto Rico was like before Columbus' arrival, archeologists have taken their clues from the artifacts left behind by various waves of cultures, often at burial sites and refuse piles. Each of these cultures traveled to Puerto Rico, reached its cultural zenith, and was then overtaken by the next wave of human arrivals. Sifting through the various layers of artifacts, Caribbean archeologists have been able to create a timeline of successive immigration patterns, consisting of waves of people who traveled from the Yucatan Peninsula of present-day Mexico and Central America and from the Orinoco River basin of South America. These immigrant groups arrived in Puerto Rico, often interacting with those who came before them, adopting their ways and introducing others, until the arrival of Europeans in the Greater Antilles drastically altered the course of Puerto Rican history.

In addition to archeology, another method historians use to understand indigenous cultures of the past is to study the language patterns and cultural characteristics of the present-day people who are thought to be most closely related to them. These specialists, called ethnohistorians, have been able to trace the cultural legacies of the island's earliest communities to many present-day traditions still upheld by Puerto Ricans on the island as well as by Puerto Ricans living in the United States. They also study the cultures of indigenous peoples who they think are related to past Puerto Rican people. These relatives of past Puerto Rican indigenous cultural groups now live on other Caribbean islands and in Central America and South America.

Ethnohistorians also study written records and descriptions of indigenous languages and other cultural elements left behind by the early European explorers to Puerto Rico. Though these records were once considered the most accurate evidence of indigenous history and culture, contemporary historians tend to acknowledge that these written records, although valuable, must be examined within the context of the motivations of those who wrote them and may not in fact present an accurate portrayal of the beliefs and practices of the Native Peoples of Puerto Rico.

Among the most recent, and perhaps the most significant, findings in the area of Pre-Contact Puerto Rican studies is one that doesn't come from historians but from scientists. Using DNA evidence collected from the skeletons of Taínos and comparing it to the DNA of their present-day descendents, geneticists from the University of Puerto Rico have drastically altered long-held assumptions about how many Taínos and Caribs survived the early colonial era.

Thanks to the work of these scientists and historians, we are beginning to get a clearer picture of what life was like for the early Puerto Ricans prior to and just after Contact with the first waves of European colonizers.

EARLY HUMAN SETTLEMENTS (2000–200 BCE)

Long after its neighbors hosted small pre-agricultural communities, Puerto Rico remained uninhabited by humans. Cuba and Hispaniola (the island that now consists of Haiti and the Dominican Republic) were inhabited starting in 4000 BCE, or possibly earlier. By contrast, human inhabitants traveling by sea did not settle in Puerto Rico until about 2000 BCE. Based on the archeological evidence, these first Puerto Rican people had originally lived in the Orinoco River basin of South America in what is now Venezuela. They traveled north by boat, stopping first at the islands of the Lesser Antilles to the south. According to the archeological record, it appears that many members of this South American tribal group settled on other islands, such as Trinidad and Grenada, even as their companions moved ever northward settling most of the Caribbean islands, including Puerto Rico. These first Puerto Ricans settled in the island's mangrove swamps, which provided abundant sources of food and shelter from the sea.

It seems likely that a second group of people, traveling east from the Yucatan, disembarked first in Cuba, then sent members of its clan to settle on the northern end of Puerto Rico. Both groups, the South American arrivals in the south and the Mesoamerican settlers to the north, lived in caves near mangroves. Historians refer to both of these groups as "archaic," "aceramic," or "pre-ceramic," all terms that simply mean that they did not produce ceramic objects. They also had not developed a system of agriculture. However, it should not be assumed that they were "primitive" or without skills. For example, there is evidence that they were effective fishermen. Their small communities managed to survive for thousands of years, growing into communities of about 25 to 30, the maximum sustainable number without an agricultural food source. In addition to fishing and gathering shellfish, they hunted turtles and manatees. Since slightly different species of animals were available for hunting on each island, the various island communities traded goods and foodstuffs regularly. Thus, they were also expert inter-island travelers, who built seaworthy canoes and established trade routes. They also created implements for hunting and food preparation by carving shell, bone, and stone. The descendents of this aboriginal group, called Guanahatabeyes in Cuba or the Culture of the Crab because of the large amount of crab remains found in their refuse piles, were still living in remote sections of Cuba and Hispaniola when the Spanish arrived thousands of years after these people initially arrived on the shores of the Caribbean Islands.

By about 500 to 200 BCE another group of settlers, this time with agricultural skills, arrived from South America, settling in Puerto Rico and nearly every other island in the Caribbean, mingling with the previous cultures and to a large extent overtaking them. These sophisticated potters, called the Saladoid people, left behind a wealth of artifacts. The artifacts' white-on-red color scheme and cross-hatched decorations create a link to similar cultures in Venezuela from around the same era. This red-and-white, crosshatch pattern abruptly disappears in the archeological record prior to the Taíno flourishing. Though the pottery that follows is technically advanced and elaborate, the abandonment of the red-and-white pattern has sparked debate among archeologists, with some arguing that the change in technique indicates the influx of a new immigrant group that merged with the Saladoid people and others speculating that this shift in pottery decoration represents the arrival of an entirely new ethnic group that retained little of the Saladoid culture.

This group of people is often referred to as Igneris, or the Hacienda Grande people because the first and most extensive cache of their artifacts was found at Hacienda Grande, a settlement founded at the same site much later by Puerto Rico's first governor, Juan Ponce de León. Among the artifacts found at Hacienda Grande and other sites were vessels for storing food. The archeological record of the Saladoid people in Puerto Rico gains in sophistication and skill from 500 BCE to about 1200 CE. Growing numbers of archeologists in the 1990s and 2000s have speculated that the Saladoid people were not a new wave of immigrants at all, but that this highly accomplished culture evolved from the earlier pre-ceramic society. This hypothesis hinges on the argument that the people of Puerto Rico and other Greater Antilles inhabitants gained their cultural influences, not from an influx of new arrivals from South and Central America, but from trade and cultural interaction with cultural groups from these areas. This chapter adheres most closely to the interpretations of leading, long-established historians, such as Irving Rouse and Ricardo Alegría, who believed the Saladoid were a new group, albeit influenced by their more ancient neighbors.[1]

TAÍNOS: "THE GOOD PEOPLE"

By 1200 CE, the Saladoid people had reached a level of cultural flourishing that has been attributed to the rise of the Taíno culture. There is some speculation that the Taíno were not descendents of the Salaloid people at all, but instead represented yet another wave of immigrants from Mexico and Central America to Puerto Rico and its neighboring islands throughout the Caribbean.[2] These new settlers, historians argue, brought customs that have much in common with the Maya, particularly in the society's emphasis on a ball game played on elaborate ball courts. These ball courts have been found throughout Mesoamerica and the Caribbean. In any event, it is unclear who the Taíno were ethnically. Were they a combination of the pre-ceramic fishermen who first inhabited the island and the skilled Saladoid farmer-potters who came to the island 1,500 years later? Or were they more closely related to the Maya?

Whatever their origins, archeologists pinpoint the emergence of the Taíno culture with the appearance of ball courts, the establishment of highly populated communities, intensified and highly effective agriculture, and the emergence of elaborate religious artifacts called three-pointers. The period from 1200 to 1490 CE—right before the first contact with Europeans—is called the Taíno Florescence (historians define a florescence as a period of cultural accomplishment).

During this time, the Taíno people were the dominant cultural group throughout the Greater Antilles (present-day Cuba, Jamaica, the Dominican Republic/Haiti, and Puerto Rico). Taíno groups located on each island visited one another frequently. In fact, Puerto Rican Taínos visited their counterparts in Hispaniola on a daily basis. Their elaborately carved, well-crafted canoes held up to 150 people and could travel swiftly and safely across the Mona Pass, which separates Puerto Rico from Hispaniola. The Puerto Rican Taínos engaged in trade with Taíno and other Native groups on other islands and with peoples from the coast of South America.

Lifeways

The Taíno were sophisticated and efficient farmers, who were able to feed and sustain a large population by cultivating a wide variety of foodstuffs, including corn, fruit, sweet potatoes, beans, squash, peanuts, and chilies. They also cultivated medicinal herbs and tobacco. Their staple food was cassava (also called manioc or yucca), a tuber that they grew in mounds. Cassava is poisonous and to eat it safely, the Taíno developed a method for boiling away and discarding the poisonous water contained in the raw harvested plants. Cassava was eaten in a variety of ways, most commonly as bread baked on a clay griddle.

Taínos were effective at gathering food from the water as well as from the land. Though they did not forge metals, they used hooks made of bone and shells, woven cotton nets, and bow and arrows to catch fish in the sea, rivers, and lakes. They also sometimes threw poison made of the barbasco plant into the water, where it asphyxiated the fish, causing them to die and float to the surface where the Taíno could easily gather them. This poison did not harm humans and did not permanently harm the water.

As their agricultural productivity increased, the Taíno were able to concentrate their efforts on creating and refining their complex political system and creating impressive cultural artifacts. Freed from the ardor of subsistence farming and hunting, Taíno artists, mostly women, discovered new and innovative ways to create and decorate ceramic objects, while male artists reached artistic heights in the carving of wood and stone.

Most Taínos wore no clothes but they anointed their skin with natural oils from plants found on their islands, which protected them from bug bites and from rashes and other skin irritants from contact with poisonous plants. Some of these oils gave their brown skin the "red" appearance that the Spanish chroniclers noted and that has been erroneously attributed to the Native peoples of the Americas ever since.

In addition to anointing their skin, unmarried women wore cotton headbands, while married women wore short cotton skirts. All Taínos wore ornaments, including necklaces and belts, crafted from gold and shells. They also wove cotton hammocks (*hamacas*) for sleeping.

The Taíno language was rich and expressive and the Spanish and English languages retain many words from it, including barbecue, canoe, hammock, hurricane, and tobacco. In addition, many Puerto Ricans still use the Taíno name for their homeland—Borinquen or Borikén, which means "Land of the Noble Lord"—and refer to themselves as Boriqueños or Boricua. The word "Taíno" means "the good people." In his correspondence to King Ferdinand and Queen Isabella of Spain, Columbus described Taíno as the sweetest, most gentle language he'd ever heard spoken.

Politics

Taínos were divided into two classes, the ruling *nitaínos* and the *naborías* or laborers. They lived in large communities of as many as 2,000 called *cacicazgos*, which were ruled by a *cacique*, a chief from the ruling *nitaíno* class. Some historians have speculated that the *naborías* may have been the descendents of the earlier pre-agricultural inhabitants and the *nitaíno* the remnants of the conquering Saladoid. Whatever their origins, it is clear from the early post-Contact reports that the Taíno thought of themselves as a single unified people by the time the Spanish arrived.

Each Taíno village was built around a central plaza used for ceremonial events, often with an adjacent ball court. The *cacique's* house, called a *caney*, was placed in a central position in the plaza, and the other villagers' dwellings, called *bohíos*, were more modest and built in a circle surrounding the plaza, ball court, and *cacique's* home. *Caneys* were large and rectangular, while *bohíos* were round. Each village contained about 20 to 50 *naborías* houses made of wood with thatched roofs and dirt floors. Several related families lived in each house and there were no partitions between families. There may have been as many as 100 of these communities (or as archeologists refer to them, "complex chiefdoms") on Puerto Rico at the time that the Spanish arrived.

Caciques determined who labored in what capacity within the community. Taking possession of all the goods produced, from crops to ornaments, the *caciques* would then redistribute them among the community members according to rank and need. The power of the *caciques* derived from their ability to control the labor of the *naborías* and not from ownership of the land. Like many indigenous American peoples, the Taíno did not view land ownership or land use in the same way that the Europeans did. Instead, the *nitaínos* in their capacity as *caciques* and shamans (or *behiques*) derived their power from their ability to communicate with the spirits of ancestors and gods, as healers and as prophets. Although each village had a *cacique*, the various *caciques* seem to have come from five to 12 main family bloodlines and the original ancestors of each of these clans were worshiped as gods, along with a number of other deities.

Chiefdoms were matrilineal, which means that the son of the mother or sister of the last chief inherited the post on the death of his uncle or brother. Women could inherit chiefdoms and there were female *caciques* in power at the time that the Spanish arrived. There is evidence that women also could serve as shamans, and possibly even warriors, once they were past childbearing age.[3] Though gender roles were somewhat fluid, women wove most of the baskets, rugs, and hammocks, and created most of the ceramic items that the Taíno are so famous for, while men planted and harvested cassava, fished and hunted for meat to supplement the Taínos' diets, carved canoes and wooden objects, and built houses for the *nitaínos* and the *naborías*.

Like the indigenous peoples of Mexico and of Central and South America, the Taíno played a ball game called *batey* using a ball made of rubber, a substance unknown to Europeans prior to Contact. *Batey* was played by teams, each representing a village. Teams were sometimes all male and sometimes all female, but never, it seems, coed. The ball game was played at festive gatherings called *areytos*, which brought villages together from different parts of the island. These occasions were central to the culture of the Taíno because they allowed the *nitaíno* members of the ruling class from various villages to interact. Because the *nitaínos* retained their ruling status by marriage, the local *cacique's* nearest relative was often the *cacique* of one of the neighboring *cacicazgos*. *Caciques* and their families traveled from one *caciczgo* to another by litter, while *naborías* traveled by foot. The ruling class used *areytos* as opportunities to work out differences between villages through negotiation, ball games, or even mock battles, which could become deadly. Attendees performed songs, dances, and pageants, which dramatized the history of the Taínos and also taught cultural values and morality to Taíno children. Members of the laboring class sat on stone embankments along the sides of the ball court, while *caciques* and their families sat on stools along the top of the embankments. At some *batey* sites, elaborate buildings stand at the top of the ball court. These buildings may have served as viewing areas for *nitaíno* families or as temples used to perform special rituals that coincided with the *areyto* festivals.

Spiritual Life

Much of what we know about the spiritual life of the Taíno comes from the observations of the early Spanish settlers, particularly from Father Ramón Pané, who was commissioned by Columbus to study the Taíno religion. His study offers a wealth of first-hand observations. Unfortunately, Father Pané and other Spanish observers from the period tended to view the Taíno religion from a Christian lens.

Traditionally, it was thought that the Taíno believed in one supreme sky god named Yucahu, lord of cassava, and a slightly less powerful goddess, called Attabeira, goddess of water and mother of Yucahu. Recently, some scholars have questioned whether this interpretation was colored by Catholic faith practiced by the sixteenth-century Spaniards who were charged with documenting the Taíno religion. For many Catholics, Christ's mother Mary, though revered, holy, and capable of acting as an intermediary between humans and the divinity, is secondary and not herself divine. The early Spanish tended to equate Yucahu with Christ and Attabeira with Mary, but many contemporary historians think that it is more likely that the two gods were equal in power, especially since Attabeira controlled water and winds, including hurricanes, a destructive element much feared by the Taíno. Some contemporary scholars have even argued that Attabeira was the primary god as God the Father is to Christ, with Yucahu representing a more approachable god to whom the Taíno prayed when they sought intervention with his all-powerful mother.

Three-pointers, the elaborately carved and decorated triangular objects that Taíno artists are most famous for, represented Yucahu or at least a means of appealing to him. Buried in the ground in hopes of encouraging a good crop, three-pointers seem to have had any number of other spiritual functions and were found in nearly all Taíno homes by the Spanish.

In addition to Yucahu and Attabeira, Pané reported that the Taíno revered 12 secondary gods who represented ancestors of the major ruling clans on the island, each of whom controlled various aspects of nature. The Taíno also worshiped scores of additional deified ancestors of important chiefs. Any and all of these gods were represented by *zemis* (sometimes spelled *cemis*), carved likenesses of the gods made of various materials: wood, ceramics, bone, or cloth. These small idols were a prevalent part of Taíno spiritual life, kept in nearly all Taíno homes by both the *nitaínos* and the *naborías* classes. Some scholars have hypothesized that this tradition, which was also common in Mesoamerica and other parts of Latin America, led to the contemporary practice of displaying *santos*, figurines of saints and especially of Mary and Christ, typically about six to eight inches high—the height of many *zemis*—in the homes of many Latin American Christians, as well as in the homes of many Christian Latinos living in the United States.

Caciques performed important public religious rituals, but it was the shaman who performed private rites, such as healings, for individual families and households. Shamans could be men if they were young or women if they were past childbearing age. Older male shamans were expected to take potent young men as protégés, teaching them to make sense of the hallucinations they induced by taking a potent herb called cohoba, made from the crushed seeds of a tree (*Piptadenia peregrina*) found in the Caribbean and Latin America. To enhance the potency of the herb, shamans fasted for days prior to a healing. Just before inhaling the cohoba seeds, the shaman would sit on an elaborately carved ceremonial seat called a *duho* and purge himself using a sacred stick to induce vomiting. He would also mix in nicotine-rich tobacco with the cohoba before ingesting the powerful powder. Then he (or she) would chant, dance, shake maracas made of dried gourds, and go into a trance to communicate with gods and ancestors who would send symbolic visions to the shaman allowing him to cure the illness or solve the problem faced by the family or community. Shamans were prominent in Taíno society, though there is some evidence that their influence in society was waning in favor of the *caciques* just prior to the arrival of the Spanish. At this time it seems that the *caciques* were taking over and performing many of the spiritual functions previously practiced solely by the shaman.

The Taíno believed in four epics for their people, which roughly adhere to what we know of their homeland and their society: a time of gods and the physical creation of their homeland, the emergence of a subsistence hunting community, the emergence of an agricultural society, and the emergence of the Taíno. Prior to the arrival of the Spanish, the *caciques* and shamans had been predicting for some time that a fifth era was coming. This fifth era would see the Taíno destroyed by a "clothed" people, ghosts from the land of the dead. When the Spanish arrived they thought the foretold conquerors had arrived. They also initially thought the Spanish were immortal and that it was useless to resist them.

ENCOUNTERS: TAÍNOS, CARIBS, AND EUROPEANS

The Taíno Battle the Carib (1450–1500 CE)

By the late 1400s CE, the Taíno were engaged in a complex, increasingly antagonistic relationship with a group of newcomers from South America called the Kalinago, or Carib. To distinguish these Amerindians from the Carib Indians still living today in South America, these people are sometimes referred to as Island-Carib. Aggressive warriors, the Carib had traveled north by boat from the Orinoco River basin of South America in what is now Venezuela. They had settled among the smaller, less densely populated Caribbean islands, overtaking the Igneri people who lived there and gradually working their way northward toward the Greater Antilles, just as so many waves of South American groups had done before. At first it appears the Carib were content to trade with the Taíno of the Greater Antilles, but by the time the Europeans arrived in the early 1490s, the Carib had begun antagonizing the Taíno by raiding their communities and taking their women as brides.

Though the Carib are famous for their skill as warriors, they were also productive farmers and skilled weavers and potters. Theirs was a hybrid culture representing the domestic, linguistic, artistic, and possibly agricultural accomplishments of their brides' Igneri culture, and the warrior traditions and navigational skills of the male Island-Caribs. The male warriors seem to have left their South American villages behind in hopes of settling new territory without taking any women or children from their homeland with them. Instead, they engaged in bridal capture. The warriors, who lived in isolation in separate dwellings from the women and children, did not have a highly developed language or culture and they often adopted aspects of the language and customs of the women they brought into their settlements, first Igneri and later Taíno. Carib men spoke a basic language they employed for trade and battle, while they allowed the women they had captured to control the practices and rituals on the domestic sphere, including child rearing. As compared to the Taíno, the Carib had a small population and were far less open and welcoming toward the Spanish. Because the Carib were mobile and transient and had not established a cultural stronghold in the Caribbean at the time of their first contact with Europeans, we know much less about their culture than we know about the Taíno. As of this writing, what little historians have surmised about the Island-Carib comes from a scant archeological record and accounts of the early European settlers. These accounts are likely biased by the Europeans' wishes to quell the Caribs' armed resistance to Spanish occupation and their desire to enslave them. At best, even accounts from the most well-meaning Spaniards are biased by simple misunderstanding and the profound cultural differences that existed between the observers and the observed. Even more than the Taíno culture, the Carib culture was radically different than sixteenth-century Iberian culture and it seems highly probable that the Spanish chroniclers misunderstood much of what they saw.[4] Working from such unreliable source material, even the most respected theories about Island-Carib culture are largely conjecture.

Ironically, perhaps because they were feared or because they were an enigma, the Carib made a big impression on the Spanish. The entire region of the Caribbean bears their name and the word *cannibal* is derived from the word Carib. In fact, in Spanish *caribe* is a synonym for *cannibal*.

The most instructive source of information about the Island-Caribs comes from studies of their South American counterparts, the Carib of eastern South America, who today live peacefully side-by-side with Arawak tribes in Guyana, Suriname, and French Guiana. There they practice the traditions the Spanish observed among their Island-Carib kin more than 500 years ago: the men employing their simple trade jargon language and the women and children employing a more robust language within the domestic sphere. When boys come of age and join the men in the male residence, they abandon their more complex language forever and adopt the warrior language of their fathers.

In some ways the Carib were more egalitarian than the Taíno. There was only one class among the warriors, who elected temporary chiefs to carry out trade and military missions. After the mission, the chief would relinquish his leadership role. However, this egalitarianism extended to class and leadership among only the men. The Carib display none of the gender equity evidenced by the Taíno, and in fact, even today, the Carib require the women of their tribes to behave in a subservient manner toward the male warriors.

The Igneri women, now Carib brides, created pottery and kept *zemis* in their homes in a very similar fashion to the Taíno. They also wove baskets and hammocks. Brewing and consuming beer held an important social and ceremonial role among the Carib, particularly at gatherings between adjoining villages where they planned military actions and elected mission leaders. The Carib preferred surprise attacks with well-crafted, deadly weapons, including long bows, blowguns, poison arrows and darts, and a noxious gas produced by smoking hot chili peppers.

By the 1450s, the Carib were the dominant culture on several islands of the Lesser Antilles and were attempting to settle in the Greater Antilles, including Hispaniola and Puerto Rico. In response to the Carib incursion, Taíno villages located near bodies of water began building observation towers so that they could spot the Carib warships and defend themselves from the increasingly frequent Carib attacks.

THE SPANISH INVADERS

The Spanish Settle Hispaniola

Christopher Columbus encountered the Taíno on Hispaniola on his first voyage to the Americas in 1492. He described them as peaceful and was immediately impressed by their two-tiered social-political system, which reminded him of Europe's own class distinctions. He was also impressed by the gold ornaments the Taínos wore as necklaces and belts. From this time forward, Spain would accord a degree of deference to the *nitaínos* chiefs and their families, treating them in a manner similar to the way a conquered vassal or lord might be treated in Europe.

On his return to Spain, Columbus brought six Taínos back to Europe, where he presented them at the court of Queen Isabella of Castile, the sovereign who had paid for his voyage, and her husband, King Ferdinand of Aragon. Their daughter, the future Queen Juana, was also in attendance. The princess and her parents acted as godparents when the six Taínos were baptized in the Christian faith. All but one of the Taínos returned with Columbus on his second voyage to the Americas.

After Columbus' first voyage to the Americas in 1492, some European sovereigns questioned whether these new lands rightfully belonged to Castile. In 1493, Pope Alexander VI bestowed control of any future discoveries in the Americas to the "Catholic Kings" as Ferdinand and Isabella were called. Therefore, in the eyes of the subjects of Castile and Aragon, the territories of North, South, and Central America and the Caribbean were Spanish by divine right.

The king and queen placed seventeen ships under Columbus' command for his return to the Americas. They instructed him to create settlements, develop a trade relationship with the Taíno, educate them in the Christian faith, and construct mines to extract the gold they believed must be abundant on the islands as evidenced by the Taínos' ornamental belts and necklaces.

In the fall of 1493, as he sailed toward Hispaniola, Columbus and his small landing party stopped at the Carib-occupied island of Guadeloupe, where they were hailed by a small party of Taíno women and children who said they had been captured by the Carib. They asked the Europeans to take them back to their home and guided them to a land that Columbus described as beautiful, an island the Taíno called Borinquen.

No one is quite sure where Columbus landed on November 19, 1493. Some say Aguada or Aguadilla, in the northwest corner of the island, but the best candidate is considered to be Boqueron Bay near Cabo Rojo on the southwest side of the island. Columbus decided to name the island San Juan Bautista.

The early Spanish chroniclers reported that the coasts of Puerto Rico (and Hispaniola) were densely populated with Taíno people. In their reports, they described valleys that were cleared, extensively farmed, and dotted with highly complex communities, each headed by a *cacique* or chief. They noted that the villages along the coast had several hundred inhabitants.

Almost immediately after the arrival of the Spanish, the Taíno began forming alliances between their chiefdoms to resist the Spanish. However, the Spanish routinely referred to the Taíno as peaceful and blamed any resistance they encountered on the Carib. In contrast, they described the resistant Carib people as savage human flesh-eaters, "cannibals." This allowed them to obtain leave from their monarchs to enslave the Carib as enemies of the king and queen and make them prisoners of war. This oppositional narrative of the good, cooperative Native versus the bad, rebellious, and dangerous Native would influence European policy toward Americas' indigenous peoples for centuries to come.

Because the slave industry provided income and free labor for the *conquistadores'* search for gold, many historians believe that Carib brutality was exaggerated. For example, there is little archeological evidence that the Carib ate human flesh for sustenance. They may have ingested small portions of the most valiant of their enemies in a ceremony that honored the warrior's spirit and allowed it to pass along to his victorious enemy. Both Taíno and Carib kept the bones of ancestors and revered enemies in their homes as talismans. Some historians have even speculated that there was no actual ingestion of human flesh at all, and that the legend of the Carib as cannibals is merely a misinterpretation of rituals surrounding the preservation of human remains. It is likely that rebellious Taíno were labeled as Carib to justify their enslavement. In a similar fashion, Spanish clergy eager to justify their efforts to repress the Taíno religion reported that the *zemis* were actually representations of the devil and destroyed hundreds of them.

In 1494, one of Columbus' officers, Antonio de Torres, returned from the Caribbean to Castile with a small number of enslaved men, women, and children, all of whom were described as Carib in the communication from Columbus that de Torres conveyed to the queen. By 1495, de Torres had returned to Castile with 500 more slaves whom he described as rebellious Carib captured during an attack. Because the Carib did not take children or women along on attacks and because there were at that time no Carib villages outside of the Lesser Antilles, the "Carib" slaves transported to Europe on these early voyages from the New World were almost certainly Taíno.

That same year Queen Isabella formed a commission of jurists and clergy to determine whether the indigenous people of the Caribbean could be enslaved. The commission found that the people of the Caribbean were free and could not be enslaved.

In 1503, Queen Isabella issued the first *repartimiendo*, or distribution of the Taíno into divisions of labor to be used on each *encomiendo*, or parcel of land decreed to individual settlers. This original *repartimiendo* barred the Spanish from enslaving the Taíno, but allowed them to demand that the *caciques* supply the settlers with laborers in exchange for instruction in the Catholic faith. Because the Spanish saw the Taíno ruling class as vassals to their sovereign, they considered the *encomiendo* system justified. After all, feudal lords in Europe could be required to share the labor of their subjects for the greater good of a king or queen. In reality, however, the system crippled the Taíno culture, leaving no time for the Taíno to grow their own crops. The colonizers did not adhere to the rules the queen had established to guide the treatment of the workers and in essence the *encomiendo* became a system of slavery, with no difference in treatment for the Taíno and Carib, who could be legally enslaved according to royal decree as enemies of Spain. The settlers twisted the intent of the *repartimiendo* system, using it to justify their demands for labor, to punish laborers whose efforts did not satisfy them, to claim island resources as their own, and to impose their own religion and customs on the indigenous people of the island. The stage had been set for the near-annihilation of the Taíno culture.

In the years to come, many Spaniards who visited the colonies would protest this situation, especially Bartolomé de las Casas in *A Short Account of the Destruction of the Indies*. He reported that less than 10 percent of Taíno laborers managed to live more than three months under the forced labor conditions of the Spanish mines and farms. The first *encomiendo* devastated the Taíno of Hispaniola, where most of the earliest Spanish settlements were concentrated.

The Spanish Settle Borinquen

In 1505, Vicente Yáñez Pinzón, who captained the *Niña* on Columbus's First Voyage, was named captain of San Juan Bautista. It was expected that he would settle the island; however, aside from symbolically sending a few fellow *conquistadores* to the island with a herd of goats and sheep, he made no attempt to do so. In 1506, he gave his captaincy to Martín García de Salazar, who also showed little interest in colonizing San Juan Bautista. Although it appears he landed on the island in 1506 with five ships and 100 men, it is unclear whether they stayed or simply sailed back to Hispaniola. Certainly they established no permanent settlement. His captaincy expired in 1507.

In 1508, Juan Ponce de León, an ambitious conquistador and military veteran, was selected by King Ferdinand and the territorial governor, Nicolas de Ovando, to settle Puerto Rico. After landing on the southeast coast of the island on August 1, 1508, he and about 50 settlers established mining and farming operations on the southwestern coast, where he founded the city of San Germán; in the northeast, he established the village of Caparra, which would later be moved about 10 miles north to the more easily defensible inlet that became the capital city of San Juan. De León's *encomiendo*, or community of enslaved Taíno and Carib Indians, lived in a village called Hacienda Grande, east of the Caparra settlement, where he put them to work seeking gold. (Hacienda Grande is now an important source of archeological information about the post-Contact living conditions of the indigenous people living on the island in the *encomiendo* era and has also provided important Saladoid-era findings.)

A few months before arriving on the island, under the orders of Governor Ovando, Ponce de León had taken part in a brutal massacre designed to quell dissent among the Dominican Taíno. After ambushing at least 600 Taíno in the house of a local *cacique*, Ovando had ordered his men to attack the men and women in the house savagely so as to inflict dramatic stab wounds. He then ordered his men to drag the Taíno bodies out to the square, ostensibly to be counted, but in fact the entire endeavor was staged to instill fear in the surviving Taínos.

News of de León's part in this massacre accompanied him to Puerto Rico and initially many Puerto Rican *caciques* tried to accommodate the new European governor. Because the Taíno shamans had long predicted the arrival of a clothed, immortal group of ghostly newcomers, many thought it was futile to resist the Europeans' demands for labor and goods. However, as the settlers became more numerous and more brutal, the Taíno became desperate to gain their freedom. Disease and starvation were beginning to take their toll on the Taíno women and children, and the men who were, encumbered with the *encomiendo* were becoming increasingly determined to escape the Spanish yoke so that they could work their own lands and feed their families.

In 1510, Chief Urayoán decided to test the belief that the Spanish were immortal by having his subjects drown a Spaniard named Diego Salcedo as they were carrying him across a river on a litter. To ensure that Salcedo did not come back to life, once on shore they watched over his body until it began to decay. Once the Taíno learned that a Spanish man could be killed, several prominent chiefs from across Puerto Rico (and possibly the Virgin Islands) met to plan an attack against the hacienda of Cristóbal de Sotomayor, a particularly brutal landowner and adviser to Ponce de León. In the raid, the Taíno rebels killed as many as 200 settlers, including Sotomayor and his son, at Villa Sotomayor and other settlements.

After this uprising, Ponce de León led a troop of fewer than 100 men to face what turned out be 11,000 armed Taíno men. De León was an experienced soldier who as a teenager had taken part in Spain's conquest of Granada, the last Moorish stronghold in Spain. Though he quickly realized he could not achieve immediate victory against the large indigenous forces, he also knew that he faced an enemy unaccustomed to joint military action. Though he was vastly outnumbered, he managed to escape defeat by killing the Taíno leader, Chief Agueybana, and instigating confusion among the loosely affiliated Taíno troops. He retreated and returned to Caparra, where he devised a plan to weaken the Taíno force. First, he offered amnesty to any leaders who wished to lay down their arms. The loss of Chief Agueybana and the surrender of some of the most powerful *caciques* on the island left the remaining rebels disorganized. Some took cover in the Cordillera Central mountain region, occasionally carrying out attacks against the settlers, but largely retaining their way of life in isolation, attempting to avoid detection and inscription into the increasingly harsh systems of *encomiendo* and slavery. Meanwhile, Ponce de León chased down known rebels and branded their foreheads with the letter "F" in honor of his patron, Ferdinand of Aragon.

By 1512, many of the Taíno men who chose to revolt against the *encomiendo* system escaped and joined their former enemies the Carib to fight the Spanish. That year, the newly allied Taíno-Carib warriors repeatedly attacked the settlement of San Germán on the western side of the island. Columbus' son, Diego, now governor of the Indies, appointed Cristóbal Mendoza governor of Puerto Rico and charged him with quelling the revolt. That same year, the Laws of Burgos were enacted in an effort to safeguard the well-being of the Taíno laborers participating in the *encomiendo* system and to set procedures for how chiefs, children, and women were to be treated by the settlers. The colonists found new ways to use the Laws to justify their harsh treatment of the laborers. To make matters worse, even the easily manipulated Laws of the Burgos did not apply to the "Carib" slaves, which was further incentive to label any indigenous people as Carib.

In 1513, Mendoza led a bloody campaign against the rebel Taíno and Carib, which provoked the Taíno to destroy San Germán. From there they rowed their warships around the island to San Juan bay. They set fire to Caparra and attacked the town of Loíza.

Although the Taíno and Carib managed occasional victories, because they did not forge metals, their weapons were no match for the Spanish during these years of open rebellion. But perhaps even more devastating than the Europeans' weapons were their diseases. The Taíno had no immunity to many European ailments, particularly small pox and influenza.

Escaped Carib slaves and Taíno workers who were not killed in battle or by disease often committed suicide on returning home to find that their families had died of yet another rampant difficulty facing the Taíno, starvation. During the first few decades after 1493, many Taínos who could not escape the *encomiendo* and who could not bear living as slaves committed suicide by hanging or by drinking unprocessed poisonous cassava juice. At the same time, some Spaniards insisted that the villages assigned to them under *encomiendo* be forcibly moved and consolidated so that the workers were more easily accessible. This practice further reduced the population as it placed women and children, in addition to male laborers, in the vicinity of deadly European diseases.

During the time that the Taíno men were bound into the *encomiendo*, Taíno and Carib women were taken as brides by Spanish settlers. Although there was mingling of European and indigenous (and later African) bloodlines throughout the Americas, the situation was slightly different in the Spanish colonies, where the colonists did not have the same taboos against interracial marriage that later European settlers, such as the English and the French, had. According to the census of 1514, 40 percent of Spanish settlers had Indian wives. These women and their children were automatically exempt from the *encomiendo*.

By 1518, the Spanish were alarmed at the rate at which the Taíno population was dwindling and many colonial leaders tried to establish some autonomy for the Taíno in hopes of restoring their spirits and their numbers. It was too little, too late. The population continued to decline. In 1542, Spain freed the slaves of indigenous ancestry, including the Taíno and Carib, but by then many had died and many of those remaining had become assimilated into the Spanish colonial culture. The Taíno civilization ceased to exist. Or so it was believed.

THE LEGACY OF THE TAÍNO

Recent archeological evidence indicates that some Taíno and Carib managed to forge a joint culture and went into hiding, particularly in the interiors of many of the Caribbean islands. At the same time, DNA testing suggests that nearly all Puerto Ricans have some Taíno and/or Carib ancestry, at least through their maternal ancestral line, which is measured through mitochondrial DNA (or mtDNA). In fact, Amerindian mtDNA has been found in higher concentrations than African or European mtDNA in a cross section of Puerto Ricans, a reversal from what most historians maintained just 10 to 15 years ago.

The archeological and genetic data indicate that more Taíno and Carib than originally thought may have survived long enough to contribute to the Puerto Rican gene pool. The DNA findings date to the discovery of four skeletons in the 1980s at a construction site in Arecibo. The skeletons were dated to 645 CE by experts from the University of Puerto Rico, where geneticists, chiefly Juan Carlos Martínez Cruzado, conducted carbon dating and DNA testing. Dr. Martínez Cruzado compared the genes of the skeletons with samples from the Puerto Rican population on the island and on the mainland of the United States. The findings called into question assumptions long stated in nearly all history books and textbooks about Puerto Rico, namely that the Taíno and Carib were wiped out early in the 1500s and that the Taíno had almost no impact on the ethnicity or even the culture of the people who call themselves Puerto Ricans.

Dr. Martínez Cruzado is convinced his findings prove that bands of Taíno-Carib rebels survived by hiding in sparsely populated pockets of the island until their recent emergence as locally and federally recognized tribes, and that their ancestors who did not flee Spanish rule had a significant impact on the gene pool of the African- and European-descended people of Puerto Rico. In fact, there were higher traces of Amerindean mtDNA (61 percent) than African (27 percent) or European (12 percent) genetic material in the blood samples of contemporary Puerto Ricans living on the island and in the United States. The test sample included individuals who identified as Taíno and those who did not. Evidence of Amerindian mtDNA was high for both groups. Research using the skeletal remains is ongoing and supported by the U.S. National Science Foundation. It seems likely that these findings will lead to a reassessment of many historical and cultural assumptions about Puerto Rico and its people.[5]

In addition to DNA research, archeological research focusing on post-Contact domestic customs indicates that the Taíno women who married Spanish settlers, as well as those who married enslaved and freed Africans, maintained many of their traditions into the colonial era. These marriages resulted in a cultural heritage among today's Puerto Ricans that is strongly European, African, and Carib-Taíno.[6] Further, indigenous influences are more evident among Puerto Ricans than any other Caribbean population, according to ethnohistorians, because there were more Taínos living in Puerto Rico than any other island pre-Contact save Hispaniola, where the indigenous population was quickly decimated. Taíno and Carib cultural influences can be found on all the islands of the Greater Antilles, but these influences, particularly linguistically, are strongest among Puerto Ricans.

Due to improved scientific methods and to the extensive archeological research currently taking place throughout the Caribbean, Pre-Contact Puerto Rican history is undergoing a period of exciting discovery and transition. The old narrative of the island's origins—namely that the Taíno are long extinct, their culture effectively wiped from the face of the earth for nearly 500 years—is being revisited and the cultural legacy of the Taíno and Carib reassessed. Today's historians agree that the island's indigenous past has played a significant role in the island's history and on the identity of the people who call themselves Puerto Ricans. This indigenous past is manifested genetically, culturally, and symbolically, and embracing it has served as a way to claim a unique identity apart from, and often in opposition to, Spain and the United States—the entities that have controlled Puerto Rico's fate for the more than 500 years.

3

Spanish Colony: From San Juan Bautista to Puerto Rico (1493–1800)

To understand Puerto Rico's earliest years as a Spanish colony it is necessary to understand something about the political situation of the Iberian Peninsula at the time of Columbus' voyages to the Caribbean. The Iberian Peninsula is the section of Europe that is currently comprised of the nations of Portugal and Spain. It is often said that "the Spanish" discovered America by stumbling on the islands of the Caribbean, among them Puerto Rico, but the truth is more complicated. Christopher Columbus was an Italian whose voyages to the Americas were paid for by Queen Isabella of Castile, one of several separate kingdoms in the geographic region we now think of as Spain. The ships that carried Columbus and his mostly Spanish crews to the Americas in the 1490s sailed under the flag of Castile, not Spain. Although many textbooks state that Queen Isabella's marriage to Ferdinand of Aragon in 1469 united Spain, this is not quite true either. At the time that Columbus made his voyages to the Caribbean and South America the separate kingdoms of Castile and Aragon were allied but did not constitute a single undisputed nation. This did not occur until the death of King Ferdinand of Aragon in 1516 consolidated the rule of Aragon, Valencia, Castile, and other regions of the Iberian Peninsula under his daughter, Queen Juana, and her son Charles V, the Holy Roman Emperor. Therefore, the laws of Castile governed the Spanish settlers of Puerto Rico from 1493 until those of the united Spain first held sway in 1516.

The date of Columbus' first voyage, 1492 CE, was also the date of the final stage of what the Spanish refer to as the Reconquest (or *reconquista*), the expulsion of Muslim rulers from the Iberian Peninsula. Christian nobles had been fighting to take back territory controlled by the Muslims (or "Moors") since 711 CE. The final victory came with the capture of Granada by forces fighting under the flags of Aragon and Castile in 1492. Several future *conquistadores* fought in this battle, among them a teenage Juan Ponce de León, who would become Puerto Rico's first Spanish governor. Over the coming decades, many of the soldiers who fought in the final battles of the Reconquest would be rewarded for their service with passage to the New World and apportioned land, as well as Taíno, Carib, and later African laborers and slaves.

There were many consequences of the Reconquest, including the expulsion of practicing Muslims and Jews from Aragon and Castile and the implementation of the Spanish Inquisition, a campaign to rid Castile and Aragon of religious heretics. In many instances the Inquisition served as a vehicle for expelling families of Jewish and Muslim descent who had converted to Catholicism in previous generations. In the decades and centuries to come many of these persecuted individuals would relocate to the New World. In addition, this Christian religious fervor served as a justification for extinguishing the religions and cultures of the indigenous peoples who the Spaniards encountered in the New World, among them the Taíno of Puerto Rico.

INTRIGUE AND THE STRUGGLE FOR CONTROL OF SAN JUAN BAUTISTA

The dual governance of the New World by Ferdinand and Isabella caused some confusion in the settlement of the Caribbean, especially in Puerto Rico. With two separate courts—one representing the interests of the kingdom of Aragon and one representing the kingdom of Castile—each issuing laws and orders on the settlement of Spain's newly discovered territories, it was inevitable that miscommunication and rivalries would emerge among power-hungry conquistadors. This situation became even more complicated after the death of Isabella in 1504 left Castile in the hands of Ferdinand and Isabella's daughter Queen Juana, while Aragon remained under Ferdinand's command. Ferdinand contested the right of his son-in-law Philip of Burgundy to assume the title of King of Castile. Instead, Ferdinand claimed that he should rule as sole monarch of Aragon and joint ruler of Castile along with his daughter, Juana. To complicate matters further, Ferdinand claimed that Juana was unfit to rule without a regent to guide her. Widely referred to as La Loca (or the Mad One), Queen Juana was widely depicted by her enemies as mentally and emotionally unstable, vulnerable to the manipulations of her husband and other close advisers. This impression of Queen Juana as La Loca has prevailed through the centuries, though some contemporary historians have begun to question her depiction as "mad."[1]

Many of the earliest settlers to Puerto Rico (then called San Juan Bautista) and other early Spanish settlements in the New World were low-ranking nobles or *hidalgos*. Many of the *hidalgos* who made their way to the New World were younger sons who had no substantial inheritance or wealth, since European estates were typically handed down intact to the oldest son in a noble family with very little property left over for any younger siblings. For these ambitious noblemen, the New World presented an opportunity to own property and accumulate gold of their own. In addition, the discovery of Puerto Rico and other territories by Columbus and subsequent explorers provided the opportunity for a generation of young, ambitious Spaniards of high birth and meager prospects—many of them tempered by war against the Moors—to compete for appointments to high posts and impressive-sounding titles in the colonies. To secure a coveted commission as captain of a ship sailing for New Spain or as governor of an island, a hidalgo might align with one of the many factions that existed in the courts of Aragon or Castile. This complicated patronage system led to many intrigues in the first few decades of Spain's colonization of Puerto Rico. A quick succession of governors took charge of Puerto Rico only to relinquish the office to rivals. Strategies for settlement and governance were mapped out and then abandoned, as one faction outmaneuvered the next.

Christopher Columbus, First Governor of New Spain

The Italian explorer Genoese Cristoforo Colombo (referred to as Cristóbal Colón in most Spanish texts and Christopher Columbus in English) found his way to Puerto Rico and the other Caribbean homelands of the Taíno by accident. It was Asia, and in particular "the Indies" (modern-day Indonesia), he was aiming for when he stumbled on the realm of the Taíno, which is why he assumed the inhabitants were "Indians."

Columbus was not the first European who believed that the Earth was round and could therefore be circumnavigated. In fact, he was not even the first European to successfully sail to the Americas. This task had been accomplished by the Vikings, who explored parts of Canada at least 500 years earlier.

However, Columbus was the first explorer of his era to secure the financial backing to test out a theory then held by only a handful of academics and sailors—that the Earth was round and that a quicker, cheaper, more efficient route to Asia could be found by sailing west than by traveling south around the continent of Africa. By endeavoring to prove his theory, Columbus changed history. He also miscalculated. For one thing, he underestimated the size of the Earth and therefore the distance between Europe and Asia. Most importantly, he assumed there were no great landmasses between Europe and Asia.

Columbus first tried to secure funding for his Asian voyage from Portugal. However, Portugal had grown rich from its Africa-to-Asia route and had no desire to change its trading strategy. This rejection led Columbus to seek funding from King Ferdinand and Queen Isabella. He waited six years for an answer to his request as the monarchs focused their efforts on expelling the Moors. In 1492 at the court of Santa Fe the newly prosperous king and queen, empowered by their recent conquest over the Moors, offered Columbus a contract known as the Stipulations of Santa Fe. Officially the funding for the endeavor would come from the coffers of Castile under the flag of Queen Isabella. Because Ferdinand and Isabella were not as experienced as Portugal's sovereign in trading expeditions like the one proposed by Columbus, and because, like Columbus himself, they did not expect the expedition to stumble on extensive island systems like the Caribbean, let alone two enormous formerly unheard-of continents, the Spanish monarchs were exceedingly generous in the provisions of their agreement with the explorer. Queen Isabella decreed that Columbus would be named admiral, viceroy, and governor of whatever islands or lands he discovered during his journey and that he would be entitled to 10 percent of any gold as well as any other precious metals and gems he obtained through exchange or mining, as well as control of any trade routes he discovered.

Columbus' first flotilla, consisting of three ships, the *Niña*, *Pinta*, and flagship *Santa Maria*, left the Canary Islands on September 6, 1492, and landed in the Bahamas 36 days later. Thinking he had landed in Japan or one of Asia's outlying islands, he soon continued west, hoping to land in China or India. Instead, he next landed in Cuba and then Hispaniola, encountering the Taíno and Carib, whom he called Indians, along the way. By the time Columbus returned from his first expedition, it was clear that he had discovered a new land altogether. He presented evidence of his discovery to Ferdinand and Isabella in March 1493 and was rewarded for his efforts with a larger expedition of 17 ships, which sailed from the Canary Islands in September 1493. It is believed that Puerto Rico's first governor, Juan Ponce de León, was among the 1,500 or so men who took part in this second voyage of discovery.

It was during Columbus' Second Voyage that he "discovered" Puerto Rico and claimed it for the Spanish. In November 1493, Columbus and a small crew were navigating their way through the Lesser Antilles when a group of stranded Taíno women and children on the Carib-controlled island of Guadeloupe hailed them. Once aboard, the women led the Europeans to the island the Taíno called Borinquen and which Columbus immediately renamed San Juan Bautista (see Chapter 2 for more on this pivotal encounter).

Because Columbus' discovery led to the near-destruction of the Taíno and other indigenous peoples of the New World, he is a controversial, widely criticized figure. However, it seems likely that his aim was to establish a trade relationship with the peoples of the New World, similar to the relationship that then existed between the Portuguese and certain African and Asian kingdoms. In contrast, the Castilian *hidalgos* aboard his ships planned to conquer, colonize, and control these new lands in a similar manner to the Castilian conquest of the Canary Islands in the early 1400s. This conflicting strategy led to disputes between Columbus and the earliest Spanish settlers to Puerto Rico. Further, Queen Isabella and her daughter Queen Juana issued several orders, such as the Laws of the Burgos (1512), designed to limit abuses against the indigenous peoples of the Caribbean. Though Queen Isabella's and Columbus' ideas of how the Taíno should be treated would be considered patronizing and abusive by contemporary standards, particularly in their disregard for the religious beliefs of the indigenous Puerto Ricans, nonetheless, in trying to adhere to the spirit of his sovereign's decrees calling for the Taíno people to be taught the Christian faith and given time each year to grow their own crops and feed their families, Columbus apportioned too many safeguards against outright enslavement for the liking of most his fellow settlers. His governorship of the island was frequently protested in letters to Queen Isabella and King Ferdinand written by colonists who wanted a freer hand with their Taíno-Carib laborers than Columbus would allow. In 1500, while Columbus was raising funds for an expedition in Spain, his brothers, who were acting as administrators to New Spain in his stead, were arrested and sent back to Spain in chains by their fellow settlers. During the 14 contentious years of Columbus' First Admiralcy, the Spanish Main (all of the New World under Spanish rule, including Puerto Rico) was ruled by three governors: Christopher Columbus (with his brothers often acting as his administrators as he sailed back and forth on his four New World expeditions), Francisco de Bobadilla, and Nicolas de Ovando.

When Columbus died in 1506, his son, Diego Columbus argued that the Columbus family should inherit his titles and King Ferdinand (a cousin of Diego's by marriage) and Queen Juana agreed. The First Admiral's titles were transferred to Diego Columbus, the Second Admiral. However, from 1506 to 1509, while Diego Columbus waged his legal battle to claim his father's titles, day-to-day governance of the Spanish Main in general, and Puerto Rico in particular, was carried out by settlers who did not favor the Columbus family. Among them were settlers favored by Aragon's King Ferdinand, including Juan Ponce de León.

Juan Ponce de León, First Governor of San Juan Bautista (Puerto Rico)

In 1508, while Diego Columbus was fighting to restore his father's titles under the Stipulations of Santa Fe and securing funding for a journey to the New World, the acting Governor of Hispaniola, Nicolas de Ovando, appointed Juan Ponce de León the first official governor of San Juan Bautista (Puerto Rico). De León left Hispaniola for San Juan Bautista with 42 men and established the towns of San Germán and Caparra, where he set up his own residence. De León and his fellow settlers soon established gold mines in the area surrounding Caparra and between 1508 and 1512, while Diego Columbus' attentions were focused on regaining control of New Spain, a steady stream of gold made its way from San Juan Bautista to Spain. King Ferdinand, who wished for the gradual settlement of San Juan Bautista to continue, viewed Juan Ponce de León as an effective governor and faithful servant to the crown. Despite his relation by marriage to Diego Columbus, the king had no immediate desire to remove de León from his post. Even after 1509, as Diego Columbus arrived in Santo Domingo and assumed control of the Americas under the provisions of the Second Admiralcy, Ferdinand urged him to allow de León to stay on as governor of San Juan Bautista. Diego Columbus grudgingly agreed to make de León his deputy, which allowed him to remain acting governor of San Juan Bautista. However, Diego resented Ferdinand for not upholding the Columbus family's claims to absolute control of all of the Spanish Main. In turn, Ferdinand was so concerned that Diego Columbus would neglect Puerto Rico in favor of settling other territories in the New World, that he secretly reiterated his appointment of de León as governor of San Juan Bautista in a letter. This was a highly unusual break in protocol, as the letter and the appointment should have gone through Diego Columbus as governor of all of Spain's New World territories. In addition, it could be argued that San Juan Bautista was the territory of Castile and not Aragon and that if the appointment of a governor was to be made directly by a monarch, rather than through the admiralcy, then such an appointment could only be made by Queen Juana and her husband, King Philip. In essence, by pitting Diego Columbus against Juan Ponce de León, Ferdinand was testing the power of his daughter and her husband, whose authority he was widely ignoring at home as well as in the new colonies, a situation that only complicated matters on the nascent Spanish colony.

Adding to the confusion, another hidalgo, Cristóbal de Sotomayor, also claimed that Ferdinand had named him governor of San Juan Bautista. However, Sotomayor had a great deal of respect for de León as a warrior and administrator, and he willingly took a second position to him in the governance of the new colony. Meanwhile, Diego Columbus named his ally Juan Cerón chief justice, a position similar to governor, in an effort to undermine de León and Sotomayor. Sensing that Diego Columbus was determined to oust him as governor, de León stepped aside and concentrated on running his farm and mines in Caparra. In 1510, after hearing of Ceron's appointment, King Ferdinand of Aragon and Queen Juana of Castile sent a rare joint dispatch naming de León governor and chief justice of the island. The vindicated de León sent Juan Ceron and his deputy Miguel Diaz to Spain under arrest on July 10, 1510.

Ferdinand's approval of de León only increased after his effective defeat of the Taíno Uprising of 1510 (see Chapter 2), but the patronage of the king would not be enough to keep Puerto Rico's first governor in power for long. Though de León won the war against the Taíno, he would soon lose the political battle for governance of the island. De León had many enemies among his fellow Spanish settlers and his contentious time as governor was coming to an end.

Though de León has often been depicted as a villain, responsible for orchestrating vicious massacres of Taínos in Hispaniola and for the defeat of the Taíno Uprising in Puerto Rico, it has also been argued that de León's lack of popularity with his fellow Spanish settlers was actually due to his refusal to ignore royal decrees aimed at curbing cruelty toward the Taíno and preventing their outright enslavement. In effect, some historians have argued, de León was not brutal enough in his treatment of the Taíno and Carib to satisfy the ambitions of his fellow *hidalgos*.[2] De León's opposition to moving the island's main settlement of Caparra to the location of present-day San Juan (which would eventually take place in 1521) was another unpopular stance that did not endear him to his fellow settlers. In short, his enemy Diego Columbus had little trouble finding allies in his plan to oust Puerto Rico's first governor.

In 1511, Queen Juana upheld Diego Columbus' petition granting him absolute control of New Spain. One of his first acts following this decree was to reinstate Juan Ceron as governor of San Juan Bautista with Miguel Diaz as his deputy. King Ferdinand, who must have suspected that Diego Columbus would displace de León at the first opportunity, had already written to de León ahead of time, instructing him to leave San Juan Bautista and attempt to colonize the areas north of the Greater Antilles. This led to de León's discovery of Florida in 1513. In 1515, he returned to Caparra, where despite holding many lofty titles from King Ferdinand in honor of his discovery of Florida, he held little power outside of his hacienda of Caparra. He concentrated on building up his settlement and farming his lands. In 1521, he organized a final expedition to Florida, where he died at the hands of Florida's indigenous Calusa people. (It would be another 38 years before the Spanish would establish a settlement in Florida.) That same year, after decades of squabbling, the settlement of Caparra was finally moved to its more defensible position on the inlet that is now referred to as Old San Juan. From then on, the city of San Juan would serve as the center of commerce, culture, and religious and political power for the island. Though he did not want the main commercial center to be located at the inlet, de León is credited with coming up with the name Puerto Rico (the rich port) to describe the harbor town and with changing the colony's name from San Juan Bautista to Puerto Rico in 1511, just before his ouster as governor.

Today, Juan Ponce de León's tomb can be found in a place of honor in the Cathedral of San Juan in the capital city. A statue of the governor can be found a few blocks away in the square just outside the Church of San José, facing in the direction of Caparra, his original settlement and family home.

Diego Columbus and the Second Admiralcy

After de León's ouster, Juan Ceron and Miguel Diaz returned from Spain to take control of Puerto Rico, instituting a new apportionment of Indians under the *Repartimiendo* of 1511. Feeling shortchanged, many of de León's followers simply ignored the rules governing Taíno labor and claimed indigenous people as slaves, often labeling the Taíno as Carib and therefore unlawful enemies of Spain. This allowed the settlers to disregard any laws governing the treatment of the Taíno. Queen Juana and her spiritual advisers, particularly the priests and friars of the Dominican order, tried to stem this mistreatment by issuing the Laws of the Burgos in 1512. These laws insisted that the Taíno nobles, the *nitaínos*, be treated as vassals, whose "peasants," the *naborías*, could be used for their labor only in exchange for certain services to their vassal lords, such as instruction in the Christian faith. Setting aside the patronizing nature of these laws, as well as their disrespect for Taíno spiritual traditions, it should be remembered that even these meager safeguards against the mistreatment of the Taíno were largely disregarded by the queen's colonial subjects.

In 1512, Diego Columbus visited Puerto Rico and appointed yet another governor, the warrior Cristóbal Mendoza, who implemented aggressive policies against Taíno rebels. In retaliation the rebels destroyed the settlement of San Germán and set fire to Caparra. By 1513, the Taíno crisis and other spiritual and humanitarian concerns led Queen Juana and her religious advisers to appoint Alonso Monso as the first Bishop to San Juan Bautista. His presence was a check on the absolute power that Diego Columbus and his appointed governors had exercised over the island since the departure of Ponce de León. However, Monso was unable to stop the widespread abuse of indigenous laborers and by the time of his arrival on the island in 1513 the Taíno and Carib populations were dwindling at an alarming rate. Many succumbed to hunger, illness, or suicide, while others fled to the interior to escape the conditions of the mines. If the Spanish thirst for gold was to be sated, a new labor source would be needed.

AFRICAN SLAVES ARRIVE IN SAN JUAN BAUTISTA (1517)

During the first decades of the sixteenth century, the upheaval and intrigue that had plagued the settlement of Puerto Rico by the Spanish continued. From 1514 to 1519, Sancho Velázquez served as governor. But by 1519, Velazquez, like de León and Ceron, had been imprisoned by his political enemies and replaced by de León's son in-law Antonio de la Gama.

During this tumultuous period, the event that was to have the most significant influence on the future historic and cultural development of Puerto Rico took place when ships carrying African slaves to work in the colonial gold mines and settlements began arriving in the Americas. It has been estimated that from the 1500s to 1820, four out of every five migrants who traveled across the Atlantic to the New World were of African origin.[3] The race-based African slave system was introduced in Puerto Rico in 1512 when the first slaves arrived, though the first official royal decree permitting it was issued in 1513, and the first large shipment of 4,000 slaves was sent to Puerto Rico and the other islands of the Greater Antilles in 1517.

West Africa

Most Africans who came as slaves to Puerto Rico (and the rest of the New World) were residents of West Africa. In the centuries prior to the establishment of the African slave trade to Europe and the Americas, this culturally, ecologically, and ethnically diverse region had seen several kingdoms rise, flourish, and then diminish. Among the most important of these kingdoms were ancient Ghana, ancient Mali, and Songhai. (The boundaries of present-day Ghana and Mali are not identical to their ancient predecessors.) Each of these kingdoms served as the center of a great empire in its time. Ghana had reached its zenith in the fifth and sixth centuries CE, when its borders stretched from the Niger River to the Atlantic and encompassed several urban centers. The Mali capital was the legendary city of Timbuktu, which served as a center of Islamic learning, cultural achievement, and trade in the thirteenth and fourteenth centuries. In Europe, Timbuktu was revered for its renowned university and library. All of these civilizations collapsed prior to the ascendancy of the Yoruba people, master forgers of metals, who built the kingdom of Oyo. Many Afro-Caribbean Puerto Ricans are the descendents of these and other ancient kingdoms.

As the slave trade became more lucrative, many of the emerging African nations took their payment from the Europeans in weaponry that they used to wage war on their declining, less powerful neighbors, whom they took as prisoners of war and then sold to the European slave traders. Other slaves were captured directly by Europeans financed by traders who wanted to cut out the African middlemen. Over the next 350 years, the period during which the importation of African slaves was permitted in Puerto Rico, the tribes and nations of origin among those captured varied but the brutality of their capture and transport went unchecked. Based on records kept by slave merchants, some historians have estimated that millions of Africans died during capture and transport across the Middle Passage. Mortality rates for slaves once they reached the Americas, particularly within the first year after capture, were also extremely high.

The Establishment of the African Slave Trade

Prior to the European colonization of the New World, slavery was not a race-based institution. Slavery had existed on every continent and among nearly every culture in the world for thousands of years, but most slaves were prisoners of war or debtors who could theoretically redeem their freedom during their lifetime and who retained certain lawful rights, particularly in the ancient civilizations of southern Europe and northern Africa. Prior to the implementation of the trans-Atlantic slave trade, slavery in Africa and Europe was not hereditary. The form of slavery that students of U.S. history are most familiar with was established by European settlers who believed they had a desperate need to replace the enslaved Taíno-Carib workers in Puerto Rico and other territories of New Spain with a steady supply of cheap labor. As the Taíno-Carib population dwindled—at least as a distinct population—the number of African slaves increased.

When the mines became less profitable, the need for slave labor was redirected to farms, cattle ranches, and sugar, coffee and tobacco plantations.

Throughout the New World, as plantations proliferated and the number of slaves increased, the human rights that slaves had traditionally been entitled to since the ancient periods of European and African history began to disappear. Slavery became a permanent hereditary institution based on race. The treatment of those who were enslaved or born into slavery was left to the whims of individual owners. This form of slavery, which started in the Spanishcontrolled Caribbean, quickly spread throughout the Americas and Europe, where it was adopted by Spain's rivals, including the French and English. Between them the European colonizing nations would transport between 10 and 15 million enslaved Africans to the Americas over the next 400 years.

Individuals of African descent became the majority ethnicity among Puerto Ricans by the 1530s, especially once Europeans began leaving the island to pursue opportunities presented by the discovery of rich gold reserves in Mexico, Central America, and South America. During this time, colonists began transferring their African slave labor force from the mines to their farms and agricultural enterprises, particularly cattle ranches, as Puerto Rico became a leader in the leather trade, with an estimated 100,000 cattle on the island by 1620.

Puerto Rico's stagnant economy kept its slave trade fairly small as compared to other colonies. In fact, by the 1700s most of Puerto Rico's African population consisted of those who had escaped slavery among Spain's enemies. These African people came to the island because, beginning in 1664, Puerto Rico had become a safe haven, granting asylum to any slaves who managed to escape from English, French, or Dutch colonies. In the institution's final century, from the 1760s to the 1870s, the enslaved population of Puerto Rico hovered around 10 percent of the total population, while its total African Caribbean population was much higher.

A STRATIFIED SOCIETY

In 1543, Spain ordered its colonists to free the remaining Amerindian slaves be freed. It was noted that about 60 Puerto Rican Amerindians were freed. As discussed in Chapter 2, that does not mean that there were only 60 individuals of Taíno-Carib ethnicity remaining on the island, as generations of previous histories have erroneously maintained. It simply means that there were 60 Taíno-Caribs who were either not hidden by slave owners who did not wish to adhere to the decree, had not fled to the interior, were not living as brides of Spanish colonists or African laborers, or were not free individuals of mixed Amerindian heritage. By the 1802 census, 2,300 individuals were counted as "Indios."

Perhaps because there were more free individuals of African descent living in Puerto Rico than there were slaves and because there was little stigma to interracial marriage between African, European, and Taíno-Carib individuals, Puerto Rico had a far less violent racial history than many of its neighbors. Nonetheless, a rigid class system separated various groups living on the island. Spanish-born colonists were typically at the top of this ladder, with native-born whites, or *criollos*, next. (*Criollo* is also used to refer to anyone born in Puerto Rico, whatever their ethnicity). Those of mixed race came next, with *mestizos*—those of European and Taíno-Carib descent—slightly higher on the socioeconomic scale than *mulatos* (a word used to describe a person of African and European or African and Amerindian descent that does not carry the stigma in Spanish that it does in English). Taíno-Caribs were largely exempt from the social hierarchies, as they remained secluded from colonial society, retaining their culture in the interior and interacting with dominant Puerto Rican culture as little as possible. Freed Africans were often poorer than those of mixed race and the working conditions they endured under white landowners were severe. In the 1800s, a combination of forces, including the ascendancy of the sugar trade and a resulting influx of large numbers of African slaves, race-based slave revolutions on neighboring Caribbean islands, and the simultaneous immigration of European settlers with harsher attitudes toward racial intermarriage than had been previously held by the Spanish, ushered in an era of racial tensions that would color the island's social history long after the abolition of slavery in 1873.

Race-based differences in socioeconomic status should be kept in mind when considering Puerto Rico's history. The origins of these differences as they were heightened by economic developments of the nineteenth century will be further examined in Chapter 4. Despite these tensions, it can still be argued that high rates of interracial marriage among Puerto Ricans, particularly those that took place in the island's first three centuries as a Spanish colony, mitigated some of the more profound and violent schisms among racial and ethnic groups seen in other parts of the Americas. In addition, it is not uncommon for contemporary Puerto Ricans to claim a mixed ethnic heritage of European, Amerindian, *and* African ancestry whatever their apparent ethnic phenotype.

ECONOMIC SHIFTS: FROM GOLD TO AGRICULTURE TO MILITARY WELFARE STATE

As it became more difficult to extract gold from Puerto Rico's mines, Spanish colonists began leaving the island to seek wealth in the ever-expanding frontiers of New Spain, particularly in the gold mines of Mexico. Things got so bad that in the 1530s Governor Manuel de Lando threatened death by hanging to any colonists who left for other parts of New Spain and actually cut off the feet of two colonists caught leaving the island.

Those who remained on the island turned their attention to agriculture as a source of revenue. Tobacco, sugar, ginger, and cinnamon were cultivated, harvested, and shipped to Europe, and cattle were reared primarily for use in the manufacture of leather goods. Coffee was introduced during the 1700s and for nearly a century provided more revenue than the island's other agricultural endeavors. But the island never produced as much revenue as many of Spain's larger, more resource-rich territories, and in time Puerto Rico came to be valued less for its economic assets than for its pivotal strategic role as a gateway to the Caribbean. Over the centuries, Spain spent more money fortifying Puerto Rico than it ever invested in the island's economy, and far more than it extracted from the island in trade. Ironically, it was around this time that the Spanish and the colonists began to refer to the island by the name of its largest city, Puerto Rico, meaning the "rich port." The city, previously referred to as Puerto Rico, became known by the name that had previously belonged to the entire island, San Juan. The change was gradual and no one is certain of an exact date when this exchange in names became "official."

During this period of poverty, Spain tried to encourage its colonists to remain on the island and not abandon it in hopes of seeking greater fortune elsewhere in the Spanish colonies. This meant that Spain needed to supply the inhabitants of the island, particularly the soldiers safeguarding its fortifications, with enough money and goods to make living on the island tolerable. The solution to this economic conundrum was a subsidy supplied by the crown and referred to as the *situado*.

Beginning in 1582, the *situado* paid for soldiers' wages, the upkeep of their quarters and the island's fortifications, government salaries and projects, and eventually widow's stipends and a host of other church- and state-related expenses. Over time, the *situado* became the main means by which Puerto Rico supported itself, a state of dependency that lasted for centuries. Dispensed annually, the *situado* created a system by which soldiers would spend much of the year buying goods on credit from local merchants, promising to pay them back with interest when their *situado* arrived. Needed improvements to the island's infrastructure were often postponed until the government's portion of the *situado* was provided. As time went by, many colonists became angry if the *situado* arrived later than expected or if it was seen as inadequate to the needs of the growing colony. Some settlers began to question the *situado*, claiming that it stood in the way of the island creating a self-sustaining economy of its own. Eventually, economic policies that fostered a dependent relationship between Spain and her colonies, such as the *situado*, which lasted into the early nineteenth century, would become a rallying point for a nascent independence movement.

Changing trade routes also contributed to Puerto Rico's very brief rise and long and disastrous fall as a destination for commerce. During the first half of the sixteenth century most ships coming from Spain took advantage of the trade winds to stop at Puerto Rico for a brief bit of bartering—goods from Europe in exchange for goods produced on the island—before moving on to New Spain's larger, more lucrative trading centers. However, by the end of the 1500s, the lure of the fabulous wealth made available by the conquest of Mexico and other Latin American territories was too great and merchant ships began bypassing routes that would have taken them to Puerto Rico. In addition, by this time the ships were so large and difficult to maneuver that they could not safely manage the narrow Mona Pass that would allow them to disembark in Puerto Rico. More and more ships chose to stop only in Hispaniola or some other nearby island, before voyaging to Mexico or elsewhere in New Spain. The exception to this was the tendency of some ships from the flotillas, about 20 percent from 1550 to 1650, to dock briefly in northwestern ports, such as Aguada, where officers would barter textiles and other goods for fresh fish, vegetables, and fruit for their crews. This break in the flotilla pattern led to the ascension of some of the cities on the north coast of the island. After the 1650s even this pattern had dwindled, with as few as eight commercial ships landing anywhere in Puerto Rico in any given year, hardly enough nautical traffic to sustain the island's basic needs.[4]

To alleviate this dire situation, the Spanish crown granted merchants from the Canary Islands (whose earlier conquest had served as a model for the colonization of the Caribbean) limited trading routes with Spain's Caribbean territories, including Puerto Rico. The Canary merchants routinely exceeded these mandated limits to meet the needs of the colonists, and the local governors, particularly in Puerto Rico where they were more focused on military than mercantile issues, tended to look the other way.

Spanish economic policy toward Puerto Rico was inconsistent, changing drastically from one monarch to the next. For example, Charles V, hoping to create a manufacturing base on the island to fuel economic growth, provided the island with the capital needed to construct the first sugar mills in 1546 and 1552. But by the end of the reign of Phillip II in the late 1500s, the Spanish government acquiesced to the demands of its merchant class, particularly Seville's powerful *consulado* guild, by discouraging colonists in Puerto Rico and other Spanish territories from manufacturing any goods. The merchants feared that goods could be made more cheaply by the colonists. Instead, the *consulado* pressured the monarch to have the colonists send their raw materials to Spain, where they could be used to create finished products, such as textiles, leather harnesses, farming implements, and household goods. The colonists were also seen as a captive consumer market, prohibited from purchasing goods from Spain's commercial competitors. With few options, Spanish merchants expected the colonists would be willing to pay a high price for the refined goods sent back by each flotilla. The flaw in the system, of course, is that to be a reliable consumer of luxury goods one needs a steady income. With its developmental policies in constant flux and largely dictated by the political interests of various factions who had never been to the island, Puerto Rico's economy often stagnated, leaving generations of its residents in a state of almost perpetual material deprivation.

It is not surprising that the colonists would look for alternate ways to transport their goods to unofficial markets and to access consumer goods from prohibited, less expensive suppliers.

PIRATES OF THE CARIBBEAN

Piracy emerged in the Caribbean almost as soon as Spain claimed the region and began extracting its gold. Spain's rival, France, launched the first wave of sporadic piracy, which intensified following Cortes' conquest of Mexico. From 1519 to 1521, Spain attempted to transport large amounts of gold from Mexico to Spain via the Caribbean, where mercenaries, mostly French Corsairs, often Protestants who could claim religious as well as mercenary grounds for their actions, would attempt to intercept Spanish shipments. Spain's enemies also included Corsairs from the rival Iberian nation of Basque. Loaded down with gold in larger, slower ships, the Spanish crews were no match for the Corsairs, whose swifter, more easily maneuverable crafts would run the Spanish ships down, sail alongside, throwing ropes with grappling hooks over the sides of the galleons, board, engage in battles on the decks with their crews, and then make off with large portions of the gold. Sometimes the Corsairs would ransom the crew as well, emptying the ships of personnel before burning the vessels at sea. All of this took place with the sanction of the French monarchs as well as governments from other rival nations, including Basque and England. In addition to gold, the Corsairs stole tobacco, sugar, pearls, and other goods.

Because of these attacks, Spanish ships attempted to travel by fleet between Spain and the New World beginning around 1525. *La flota*, or the flotilla, set out each January and August, landing in the New World twice a year. This meant that colonists on Puerto Rico and other islands had to make do without provisions from Europe for long periods of time and that the arrival of *la flota* carrying goods from Spain was a biannual event and occasion for celebration and social interaction.

The flotilla system was adopted to avoid financing a Spanish Navy that would patrol the Caribbean, an expense that Spain hoped to avoid. In the long run, this decision would have lasting consequences on Spain's ability to maintain control over the Americas in general and Puerto Rico in particular. In the short term, it gave rise to several waves of piracy, as private ships, sanctioned by Spain's enemies during wartime and unsanctioned during times of peace, took advantage of the vast amounts of wealth being transported across the Atlantic with almost no protection. Pirates also became wealthy by intercepting Spanish ships carrying African slaves from Africa to South America and the Caribbean, although some pirate captains freed the slaves they captured and allowed them to join the pirate crews. Documents from the time indicate that at least one-third of all pirates were African.

In 1528, the colony of Puerto Rico experienced its first pirate invasion when 60 Corsairs invaded the settlement of San Germán, burning and plundering the town's farms and mines, which had been abandoned by the families living there. As the years progressed it became clear that not only the port of San Juan, but other major trading areas, such as San Germán, would need to be fortified and guarded from piracy, as well as invading armies.

By 1552, all private merchant ships trading with Spain and carrying goods from her colonies were required to carry trained militia at their own expense. With armed men on either side, the sea battles soon became deadly. When it became clear that few private merchants were willing or able to hire their own mercenaries, Spain began levying "pirate taxes" on its colonists to pay for armed guards to sail with merchant ships carrying goods to Spain. Spanish colonists, including those living in Puerto Rico, considered this tax unfair. In their view their sovereign nation owed them the protection necessary to conduct business on the open seas and many argued that they were being victimized twice—by the pirates and by their own rulers. Such arguments would eventually feed the cause of independence.

Another issue fueling colonist discontent was Spain's insistence that the Puerto Rican merchants could trade only with the Spanish ports of Seville and Cadiz, thus limiting their ability to sell their goods to the highest bidder. As a result, some colonial merchants soon made side deals with the pirates, paying them to transport a portion of their goods to more lucrative, but officially prohibited, ports.

In addition, Spain required the colonists to purchase European goods from Spanish merchants at fixed prices. This prevented the colonists from obtaining textiles and other goods at the lowest possible cost. Soon, the pirate ships were landing on Puerto Rican shores, selling goods from prohibited manufacturing centers such as Flanders, Italy, and France at discounted prices. Far from being reviled by the locals, pirate ships were often welcomed, especially when they quietly sailed in and out of ports just out of sight of the great forts and watchful eyes of the military governors. In fact, some Spanish Caribbean governors even colluded with the pirates in return for kickbacks and bribes. Puerto Rico, in particular was dependent on the pirate trade because by the 1600s its population was so small that many officially sanctioned Spanish merchant ships did not think it was worth their time to stop at any of the island ports. In addition, the high volume of pirates operating in the north coast of Puerto Rico had made it one of the most dangerous water routes in the world. It is hard to say whether Spain's policies spurred piracy in the Caribbean in general and Puerto Rico in particular, or if the reluctance of Spanish merchants to dock in Puerto Rico was the result of piracy. What can be stated with certainty is that the people of Puerto Rico depended on the black market goods the pirates provided simply to keep themselves clothed and their homes stocked with cooking implements and other everyday household goods. For many Puerto Ricans, the pirates were seen as folk heroes, who were able to supply them with their basic needs when their government had failed to do so.

Pirate scholars divide the Golden Age of Piracy (1650–1730) into three eras, two of them in the Caribbean. During the first, 1650 to 1680, Protestant English, French, and Dutch buccaneers, many sanctioned by rival European powers, invaded Spanish ships in the Caribbean in the name of religion, but benefited from the commerce. In 1674, the king of Spain began hiring his own corsairs and privateers to patrol the waters of his colonies and to counter-attack his enemies' trading ships. In exchange for their services, these sanctioned Spanish "pirates" were allowed to keep a percentage of the Spanish treasury that they were helping to protect. This era was chaotic, characterized by sanctioned and unsanctioned pirate attacks on all sides.

The second era, during the 1690s, was centered along the African coast and Indian Ocean, and represented an era of only moderate pirate activity in the Caribbean.

In the early eighteenth century, between the second and third eras of piracy, there was a brief interruption in outlaw maritime activities, but only because adventure on the high seas in these years came in the form of sanctioned raids by privateers working for rival European powers. During the War of Spanish Succession between Spain, England, France, and the Netherlands (1715–1730), crews that had been previously designated as pirates were now officially sanctioned as privateers and were rewarded by Spain's enemies for raiding Spanish ships. Spain, in turn, sanctioned privateers to raid her enemies' ships. This was a lucrative epic for mercenaries and many young men from Europe and the colonies took to the practice of looting ships and raiding colonial settlements.

The third era of the Golden Age of piracy (1730s) took place just after the War of Spanish Succession as the now non-sanctioned pirates began attacking ships. As the official navies of all four nations (Spain, England, France, and the Netherlands) departed from the Caribbean, pirates took advantage of the absence of well-armed crewmen to attack merchant ships of every nation and the number of pirate crews multiplied. In fact, many of the pirates were former professional sailors from the four navies, now out of work. The highest percentage of these former professional seamen were English, but the crews of pirate ships were highly diverse, consisting of freed slaves, *criollos* unsatisfied with the lack of opportunity created by preference often shown to European-born colonists, biracial individuals of African, Taíno-Carib, and/or European background, and Europeans from any of a half dozen nations.

Pirate ships were not run in the dictatorial manner of most European naval ships. Unruly sailors were almost never punished using the brutal corporal methods practiced by navy officers, though in extreme cases they might be left on whatever island was nearest. Missions were decided by majority vote and every pirate sailor had an equal share in the plunder. The captain was elected by his crew and could lose his position by majority vote. The captain's share of the spoils was sometimes higher, but that share was typically voted on as well. In short, a spirit of democracy reigned on pirate ships and pirate settlements, including Tortuga off the coast of Hispaniola. In fact, some contemporary pirate scholars cite the equitable spirit championed by the pirates as a precursor to the eventual spirit of revolution and democracy that would sweep through the Americas in the eighteenth and nineteenth centuries.

The loyalties of these crews were as diverse as their crews and the relationship to the various colonies complicated. Some pirates were welcomed and revered by the settlers of Puerto Rico for providing them with needed goods and access to otherwise unreachable markets for their wares. Other pirates, who held nominal loyalty to Protestant nations even though those nations outlawed their existence during peacetime, were likely to raid Spanish settlements and were therefore feared by colonists. Thus, the residents of Puerto Rico had a complex relationship with piracy, and the island held a central place in this fascinating epic of history.

It was during this period that some of the Puerto Rican governors paid pirate captains to intercept English and Dutch ships that came near their waters. Many of these ships were carrying goods from colonies in what would become the United States from ports such as Boston, Philadelphia, etc. Famed pirate captains of this era included the Puerto Rican mulatto Miguel Henriquez and San Juan resident Pedro de la Torre. The last and perhaps most famous Puerto Rican pirate was Roberto Cofresí y Ramírez de Arellano, who started out pillaging U.S. and British ships in the late 1810s and early 1820s and was largely overlooked by Spanish authorities, who approved of his activities. Later he shifted his loyalty from Spain to independence forces and began to raid Spanish as well as other nations' ships indiscriminately. It was at this point that Spain cooperated with the United States in capturing him in 1825, when he was executed on the lawn in front of El Morro. Considered a Robin Hood figure, he is said to have shared his bounty with friends, family, and the less fortunate, and to have buried treasure near his hometown of Cabo Rojo.

FORTIFICATIONS AND INVASIONS

Though the amount of gold and other salable goods Spain received from Puerto Rico was small compared to the riches extracted from the rest of New Spain, the island was strategically important. At various points, England, France, and the Netherlands all attempted to capture the island. Beginning in 1564 Spain stopped awarding the governorship of the island to political appointees. For the next several centuries, the island was governed by military leaders, and constructing fortifications to protect San Juan and other strategic settlements came to be seen as the colony's main function and highest priority.

From the 1530s through the 1540s, the military concentrated on building fortifications around the government building now called La Fortaleza, where the island's treasury was housed. In 1539, construction of the El Morro fort began. Built on a promontory overlooking the ocean, El Morro was staffed by resident soldiers and equipped with cannons aimed at incoming ships.

Throughout most of the 1500s it is believed there were never more than about 200 men available to defend the island at any given time and most of those were not professionally trained soldiers. In 1582, a professional garrison was housed in El Morro for the first time, its salaries and upkeep provided for by the first *situado*. The face of Puerto Rico was changing from a struggling commercial colony to a strategic trophy, surrounded by fortresses and under assault by a series of foreign invading powers over the following three centuries.

In dealing with the sometimes harsh, military-style justice of the martial governors the colonists could appeal to the *audiencia*, a sort of appeals court centered in Santo Domingo (Hispaniola). This court was a check on the absolute power of the governors and also helped shape Puerto Rican concepts of governance for centuries to come. Puerto Rico's local munici-palities were run by a council, called a *cabildo*. At first those on the *cabildo* were elected and tended to support the claims of settlers over the interests of the crown. Later seats on the *cabildos* were sold by the crown to the highest bidder. These royally appointed administrators tended to hold their meetings in closed-door sessions.

One of the most famous invasions came in 1595, when a damaged gal-leon, laden with gold and precious gems took refuge on the island, its treasure temporarily stored at La Fortaleza until another galleon could be sent to retrieve it. Sir Francis Drake, one of England's most famous Cor-sairs, soon heard of the treasure and devised a plan to raid San Juan and plunder La Fortaleza. Drake was regarded as a war hero by the English for his successful service in the defeat of the Spanish Armada, after which Queen Elizabeth rewarded him for his efforts with a knighthood. But in Spanish circles he was regarded as a feared outlaw and pirate. On November 22, 1595, he arrived off the coast of San Juan with a flotilla of his own. However, El Morro had been fortified in recent years and was better staffed than the war hero expected. His ships could not penetrate the fort's defenses to reach the shore and his flagship was fired on. On November 23, Drake tried another tactic, using small launches to quietly approach some Spanish ships that were anchored in the bay outside the capital city and set them ablaze. However, the first fire was spotted by soldiers on watch in El Morro who were then easily able to spot the launches and attack them from above with battery guns. The next day, Drake attempted to boldly sail his entire flotilla into the bay, braving the cannon fire from the El Morro fort. However, the Spanish chose to sink three of their own large galleons, making entrance into the port impossible. Drake gave up and left Puerto Rican waters for good. This outmaneuvering of one English history's most celebrated naval warriors has long been celebrated in both Puerto Rican and Spanish history.

Puerto Rico experienced a closer call in 1598 when George Clifford, the Earl of Cumberland, entered Puerto Rican waters with 1,400 men, includ-ing several veterans of Drake's invasion. After a 15-day battle, Cumber-land's troops captured El Morro, forced the governor to surrender, and sacked of the capital city. However, a widespread bout of gastric fever reduced his force by half to less than 700 men and forced Cumberland to relinquish control of the city just before a large fleet from Spain arrived to recapture San Juan.

In 1625, Dutch fleet commander Boudewijn Hendriksz laid siege to San Juan as an act of war, since at the time the Dutch were enemies of the Spanish as part of Europe's vast and complicated Thirty Years War. He was able to bypass El Morro because its guns and weaponry were in disrepair at the time. His troops came ashore, capturing La Fortaleza and terrorizing the residents of San Juan. However, the Dutch were not able to defeat the troops in open battle on the shore next to El Morro and Governor Juan De Haro refused to surrender. The Protestant troops then laid siege to the city's churches and looted their holy artifacts. Cumberland's troops were forced to abandon the city less than 24 hours later and return to Dutch-controlled waters aboard ships that had been badly damaged by fire from barrages launched by troops stationed in El Morro. After burning homes and other buildings and damaging much of the city, he returned to the Netherlands with treasured possessions stolen from churches and homes.

From 1701 to 1713, during the War of Spanish Succession, the military governors expected an attack from the British to its main port. Instead, a small band of 40 Englishmen came ashore in the small town of Arecibo but were repulsed by local residents. The Treaty of Utrecht ended the war in 1713.

THE O'REILLY CENSUS (1765)—THE EMERGENCE OF PUERTO RICAN IDENTITY

With very little opportunity to make one's fortune in Puerto Rico, colonists began leaving the island to pursue opportunities in Spain's other colonies. Because of this lack of opportunity, the 1673 Census stated that the island was suffering from a lack of skilled workers: carpenters, shipbuilders, farmers, blacksmiths, etc. This deficiency in workers was partially made up over the next several decades thanks to Spain's decree that any African who found his way to the Spanish colony from a territory controlled by another European power would be considered free. In addition, indentured servants of European background also began migrating to Puerto Rico, where due to labor shortages, no questions were asked. It is largely believed that these fugitives swelled the number of inhabitants on the island to about 6,000 by 1700.

The 1673 Census also noted that there were nearly twice as many women living on the island as men. One factor that helped prevent the complete stagnation of economic development on the island was the Spanish law that allowed women to own property after a husband or father's death and to control property in the absence of their husbands or fathers. These legal provisions, which did not exist in some of Spain's rival European countries, allowed women to administer property and carry on economic endeavors started by their husbands even when they were engaged in activities in other colonies.

Spain's King Charles III was not happy with Puerto Rico's slow rate of development and in 1765 sent Alejandro O'Reilly as the Special Envoy of the Spanish King to conduct a special report. His report declared that the people of Puerto Rico were the poorest in America, and that they lacked such commonplace public works as proper roads after 250 years of Spanish rule. He also reported that smuggling, contraband trade, and other forms of piracy had been more central to the development of the island's economy than any legitimate commercial enterprises. He estimated that the value of illegal trade was ten times greater than the income earned by Puerto Ricans from legitimate commerce. He noted that many of the island's settlers were outlaws and military deserters with no skills or agricultural knowledge. O'Reilly urged the crown to eliminate many of its trade restrictions on the colonists and to encourage the emigration of Catholic settlers from other countries, particularly those with agricultural skills. Following up on O'Reilly's recommendations, Spain issued reforms designed to increase immigration to Puerto Rico and managed to increase the population from the 1765 mark of about 45,000 to more than 155,000 in 1800.

REVOLUTIONS ABROAD AND ONE LAST EUROPEAN ATTACK

The revolutionary era sparked by the North American declaration of independence from the British in 1776 and the subsequent establishment of the United States eventually sparked nationalist, anti-colonial sentiment among most of the peoples of the Americas. In the near-term, its greatest impact for Puerto Rico may have been its role in igniting discontent among the citizens of Spain's rival European nation, France. When the French citizenry declared the Rights of Man in 1789 and overthrew their king in 1792 they triggered parallel revolutionary fervor among the slave populations of their Caribbean colonies including Haiti, as the victorious slaves chose to call the island that the Spanish referred to as Hispaniola. (Today, the island that was once the most populous stronghold of the Taíno civilization is home to two distinct states—Haiti and the Dominican Republic.) Frequent skirmishes between the newly established Haitian government and rival factions based on the Spanish-controlled side of the island, as well as fighting between the French, English, and Spanish—each of them determined to recapture and control the entire island—made the governance of the Spanish-controlled portion of Hispaniola increasingly uncertain and forced the Spanish to relocate the Council of the Indies to Cuba. This change of venue created a closer political and cultural relationship between Cuba and Puerto Rico in the century that followed.

The French Revolution and the slave revolts that it triggered emboldened the English, who were eager to increase their holdings in the region after losing territory in North America. In 1795, British General Ralph Abercromby traveled to the West Indies, where he captured St. Lucia, St. Vincent, and Grenada. In 1796, he was ordered to capture Trinidad and

Puerto Rico. He quickly took control of Trinidad, but Puerto Rico presented more of a challenge than the veteran of the Seven Years War had expected. During Abercromby's two-week siege in 1797, Spain's centuries-long investment in fortifications along its major ports paid off. Unable to breach the walls guarding the capital city, Abercromby bypassed the harbor and led a small force ashore on foot. This force occupied the village of San Mateo de Cangrejos (now a neighborhood of modern-day San Juan), where the general set up headquarters in the summer home of the bishop of San Juan. Confined to the small village, the British troops soon needed to venture from their headquarters to obtain additional supplies. However, Spanish troops and local Puerto Rican militias attacked their every foray. Across the island, the Puerto Rican people, including free black men living in Loíza, voluntarily took up arms and effectively silenced communications between Abercrombie's fighting units. Soon voluntary soldiers were arriving in San Juan from every village to join forces with General Ramón de Castro's regulars. On April 30, 1797, Abercromby and his forces retreated.

As governor, General Castro took advantage of the victory, winning reforms and investments from Spain that helped alleviate some of the economic hardships the Puerto Rican people had suffered leading up to the invasion. His efforts improved economic development and governance on the island during the decades ahead. He would be the last Spanish governor to enjoy widespread popularity on the island.

Though only 200 of Abercrombie's 7,000 men had been killed, the victory still resounds with symbolism on the island, where many poems, folk legends, paintings, and statues commemorate the battle. Long seen as a defining moment in island history, the English invasion of 1797 spurred Puerto Ricans from every ethnicity and every corner of the island to unite to face a common enemy, not as dutiful subjects defending the glory of the Spanish Empire, but as patriots who had begun to think of their island home as a nation in its own right.

4

Spanish Province: Autonomy Thwarted (1800–1898)

Throughout the first three centuries of the Spanish colonial period the everyday lives of Puerto Ricans were affected by events taking place in the Caribbean and the Americas, Europe, and Africa. By the early 1800s, European conflict over trade, royal succession, and the Atlantic slave trade had left its mark on the developing culture and politics of the island. This phenomenon only intensified during the nineteenth century.

The Napoleonic Wars, for example, had long-lasting consequences for Spain's relationship with her island colony. Spain's alliance with Napoleon left her treasury depleted and her citizens too impoverished to purchase luxuries, such as leather goods, sugar, or coffee from the colonies. Thus, as the nineteenth century unfolded, the United States gradually replaced Spain as Puerto Rico's leading trading partner. The 1804 defeat of France and Spain by the British Navy at the Battle of Trafalgar left the Spanish fleet wounded, diminished, and in no position to defend its colonies or to control trading activities as it once had. By 1808, Napoleon had coerced Spain's Bourbon king, Ferdinand VII, into abdicating his throne in favor of Bonaparte's brother Joseph-Napoléon. Though the French controlled portions of Spain under Joseph Napoléon Bonaparte, most regions of the country refused to acknowledge Napoleon's brother as their sovereign and a military junta took control of most of the nation.

In the coming decades Spain's Bourbon monarchy was restored, only to have its authority interrupted and challenged by a series of internal wars sparked by disputes over succession, as well as periodic coups undertaken to end the monarchy and establish an intermittent form of constitutional republican government. Amid this backdrop, many native-born Puerto Ricans began to feel increasingly alienated from a chaotic motherland, which seemed to ignore their concerns. Many native-born Puerto Ricans, or *criollos,* believed that Spain did not accord them their rights as Spanish subjects; taxed their meager earnings to pay for European wars and wayward, inconsistent trade policies; and perhaps most galling, treated recently arrived Spaniards, called *peninsulares,* with favoritism, awarding them with land grants, tax exemptions, and lucrative government posts that were seldom awarded to *criollos.*

From Spain's perspective, past investments in its colonies, from the creation of infrastructure to defense against foreign invasion entitled the government to ask its colonial subjects for contributions and special taxes in times of crisis. By 1821, nearly all of the nations of the Spanish Main had rejected this supporting role. From Venezuela to Argentina to Mexico, most of Spain's former colonies had declared their independence from the once-powerful, now-ravaged empire, and a weakened Spain was too depleted to defeat the revolutionary armies. Nation-by-nation Spain began losing control of its territories in North, South, and Central America, and by 1826, Spain's New World empire was comprised of two small under-developed islands, Cuba and Puerto Rico. (Spain also retained control over the Philippines, Guam, and other islands in the South China Sea.)

As a consequence, Puerto Rico became a refuge for defeated loyalists fleeing from revolutionary conflicts throughout the former Spanish Main. These imperial loyalists soon joined recently arrived immigrants from throughout Europe who used their capital and business knowledge to develop Puerto Rico's economy, particularly its sugar, coffee, and tobacco industries.

The nineteenth century saw Puerto Rico evolve from a sparsely populated island of mostly mixed-race *criollos* (various combinations of African, European, and Taíno-Carib), largely getting by as subsistence farmers, to a highly stratified plantation-based economy reliant on increasing numbers of African slaves. Harsh working conditions for slaves and free laborers alike and a more rigid race-based class system characterized Puerto Rico's quickly evolving economy. Meanwhile, high rates of debt among native-born Puerto Ricans and perceived favoritism for newly arrived immigrants created new tensions with the Spanish colonial government; escalating demands for autonomy, if not outright independence, characterized island politics as the twentieth century approached.

CYCLES OF REFORM AND REPRESSION

By 1808, Spain had seen British colonists successfully fight for independence to form the United States and the French populace dismantle its monarchy. But it was the violent overthrow of the colonial government in Haiti, just across the Mona Passage from Puerto Rico, that prompted a concerned Spanish government to acknowledge calls for reforms long requested by its island subjects. In 1809, hoping to cement the loyalty of its remaining colonies through economic and political concessions, Spain's Supreme Junta invited Puerto Ricans to vote for a delegate who would represent their interests before a session of parliament to be held in Cadiz. The delegate vote was Puerto Rico's first democratic election. Only landowning men were allowed to vote. The winning delegate, Ramón Power y Giralt, actually had to be elected twice because the Junta was replaced by a new political unit called the Regency before he could leave for Cadiz. The parliamentary session, or Cortes, now hosted by the Regency government, began in 1810. Power y Giralt soon won respect among his fellow Spanish and Cuban reformists and was named vice president of the Cortes. He managed to convince the Regency government to ease trade restrictions on Puerto Rican merchants in a decree called the Rey Power, which granted Puerto Rico status as a Spanish province. He also had a hand in conceiving many of the provisions of the first Spanish Constitution, drafted between 1811 and 1812. It should be noted that in addition to trade and civil reforms, Power y Giralt also carried with him demands for an independent republic from many of the elected municipal bodies that had conferred and drawn up lists of reforms prior to the delegation's departure.

Power y Giralt's prominent contribution to Spanish history was a point of pride for most Puerto Ricans, but not all. A number of royalists, *peninsulares*, loyalist refugees from Latin America's new republics, and some of the island's wealthiest *criollos* thought that the reforms went too far. Advocating a more centralized government and continued Spanish control over trade, these powerful interests made up a conservative counter-current to the reformist, autonomous movement. Opposition between these two economic, political currents would characterize Puerto Rican politics for the rest of the century. It can be argued that this political tug of war is still the dominant theme of Puerto Rican politics, on and off the island, to the present day.

In 1814, the Bourbon king, Ferdinand VII, was restored to power. Ferdinand nullified the Rey Power and the Spanish Constitution, and imprisoned many of Spain's reform-minded leaders, despite the fact that they had fought the Bonaparte government and were partly responsible for his return to the throne. By 1815, hoping to retain what remained of a diminishing empire, Ferdinand moved to retain the loyalty of Puerto Rico and, if possible, develop its economy to help make up for the trade and resources Spain had lost in its other Latin American colonies. In August 1815 he issued the *Cédula de Gracias* (Warrant of Opportunity), which encouraged immigration to the island by granting any white settler willing to convert to Catholicism and pledge support for the Spanish king six acres of land (three acres for each slave owned) and a 10-year tax exemption. Free black and *mulato* settlers would be awarded three acres of land (one and a half acres for each slave they owned) and a five-year tax exemption. If the new settlers stayed for five years they would be invited to become Spanish citizens. Most of the Cédula's provisions remained in place until 1836. The Cédula and other reforms aimed at increasing immigration resulted in a shift in the population, as the island saw an influx of European immigrants from Catalan, Valencia, Basque, Galicia, Corsica, Ireland, and France, as well as the Canary Islands, which had been a steady source of immigration since the late 1600s. Other immigrants came from throughout Latin America and the French-, Dutch-, and English-controlled islands of the Caribbean. The decree was intended to grant unused land to immigrants, who would develop it into revenue-producing farms and plantations. In fact, the new law often deeded land that had been farmed by native-born Puerto Ricans for generations to new arrivals. Many *criollos* were now required to pay rent to the new owners or work as farmhands if they wished to stay.

By 1823, Ferdinand had spent years struggling to consolidate his power and was in no mood to tolerate reformist philosophy in Spain or overseas. After nullifying Spain's second constitution and reclaiming absolute power as monarch, he revoked Puerto Rico's status as a province, reducing her to a colony once more. Ferdinand's harsh treatment of Cuba and Puerto Rico were continued under his daughter Isabel's regency and eventual rule (she was only three years old when first crowned), as well as under her uncle, rival, and sometime pretender to the throne, Carlos, Ferdinand's brother. For the next several decades Puerto Rico would be ruled by a series of anti-reformist governors, beginning with Marshall Miguel de la Torre, who governed the island from 1823 to 1837. De la Torre resented the success of revolutionaries, particularly the popular general and folk hero Simón Bolívar, known throughout Latin America as *El Libertador*, who had defeated de la Torre's troops in Venezuela. Determined to avoid further defeat and disgrace, de la Torre implemented a series of laws designed to prevent the formation of popular uprisings. He curtailed *criollo* gatherings, devised brutal punishments for anyone who disobeyed his decrees, created a secret network of informants, and offered rewards designed to encourage citizens to spy on one another and report to him any behavior that might be construed as revolutionary. De la Torre was able to issue different laws for *criollos* than for *peninsulares* because, under Spanish law, those who were born in its colonies were defined as Spaniards, rather than citizens, unless they could prove that both of their parents had been born in Spain. This discrepancy in citizenship created a two-tiered social structure even among Puerto Rico's most successful *criollos,* placing even wealthy families who could trace their ancestry back several generations on the island below recent Spanish arrivals.

Despite the repressive measures instituted by de la Torre and the governors who followed, there was a planned uprising in 1838. The intent of the conspirators, all wealthy landowners and well-placed militia members, was to declare Puerto Rico an independent republic. Though the plot was thwarted when it was denounced by an insider close to the conspirators, this planned uprising marks a pivotal moment in the history of the island as the first fully conceived plot to end the island's colonial status.

ECONOMICS: SUGAR, COFFEE, AND TOBACCO

Despite the island's political instability and its residents' fluctuating civil rights, the economy flourished during the first six decades of the nineteenth century. By 1810, Mexican independence had ended the *situado,* just as Puerto Rico's growing sugar and coffee trades were making this stipend less necessary. Between 1814 and 1854, for example, foreign trade increased 2000 percent.[1] This period of growth has been cited as the point at which Puerto Rico's economy transformed from a colonial economy to a national economy.[2]

Puerto Rico began the century with over 150,000 inhabitants and ended it with more than 1 million. In addition to a population that was finally sufficient to develop the island's agricultural potential, Puerto Rico's economy also benefited from the chaos that followed the Haitian Revolution, which had incapacitated the world's largest sugar exporter. Puerto Rico reaped the benefits, becoming a major global source of sugar (including sugar-derived products like molasses and rum) for Europe and the United States, and enjoying three decades of favorable trade balances (it exported more than it imported). However, the seeds for the island's economic downturn were embedded in its success. As more and more of its lands were dedicated to growing luxuries like sugar, coffee, and tobacco for export to Europe and the United States, the amount of land dedicated to agriculture and subsistence farming became scarcer. Increasingly, Puerto Ricans were dependent on the United States to provide food supply.

For example, by the late 1800s Puerto Rico was importing the bulk of its rice from the United States even though sufficient amounts of rice, a major part of the population's diet, had been produced locally for centuries. Now, rice had to make way for revenue-producing coffee trees in the island's southwest region.

The 1838 vagrancy laws made it nearly impossible for rural workers to grow enough food to feed their families. The laws gave wealthy land-owners an additional tool to compel rural workers and subsistence farmers to work for them for wages insufficient to support their families if and when those landowners' slave labor force could not complete work fast enough. Additional day laborers were needed at harvest and during certain points in the sugar refining process, but it was not always worthwhile for free laborers to skip a critical day harvesting their own crops for one day's meager wages on the sugar plantations. The vagrancy law provided the landowners with a tool that compelled small farmers to do just that, often at a great cost to their families' survival. *Jornaleros* (wage workers) were defined as those with no steady income or an insufficient amount of land to support a family (approximately less than 2 acres). Those classified by the government as *jornaleros* were required to seek and accept wage work immediately. Those who did not could be jailed, fined, or required to accept work for half the going rate. In 1849, after the slave trade, though not the institution of slavery, was officially ended by Spain, Governor Juan de la Pezuela issued an even harsher version, called the *Reglamento de Jornaleros* (Workers' Regulations) or the "law of *libreta*," which required wage workers to carry a passbook, or *libreta*, with them at all times. The passbooks carried notations from landowners and could be checked by government officials at any time. Officially, the intention was to prevent vagrancy, but in fact the *libreta* became a way for the landed class to track every aspect of workers' lives, from wages to debts. Because the island's uneducated workers were required to purchase food and other necessities from plantation-owned stores with money that was subtracted from their wages, many workers lived in a constant state of debt and dependency. Many plantations issued vouchers redeemable at their own stores rather than currency, thus cementing their workers' indentured status.

By 1850, the European market was purchasing less raw cane sugar and more refined beet sugar, which could be grown and manufactured in Europe. In addition to encouraging the spread of the slightly less profitable coffee industry, the growth of the European beet sugar market increased Puerto Rico's reliance on the United States as its main trading partner, which remained strong throughout the Civil War when the United States' own sugar industry was disrupted. In fact, times were so good that several Puerto Rican plantation owners over-speculated and had to sell their land after the war was over because they had defaulted on their loans. Because *peninsulares* and other immigrants tended to own shops as well as land, they weathered the fluctuations in the sugar markets better than the *criollo* planters. Also contributing to the debt problem was Spain's policy of prohibiting the establishment of banks on the island. This policy meant that private merchants provided the only means of obtaining credit. Failure to repay a debt within two years required the forfeiture of the debtor's land. By the late 1860s, the bulk of the sugar cane-growing lands were held by *peninsulares*, and a large number of once-wealthy *criollos* were in debt. In addition, small-scale subsistence farmers were having a tougher time holding on to their own lands and free white and black laborers were facing extreme poverty as well. The nature of sugar cane production encouraged the importation of more African slaves than ever and the large-scale operations of cane harvesting and milling created grueling and dangerous working conditions and tended to promote brutal treatment of slaves by overseers to keep production rates high. The Puerto Rican sugar industry was particularly labor-intensive because Spain prohibited its colonies from investing in manufacturing equipment. Spain's colonial model for the past three centuries had been based on restrictions designed to extract Latin America's natural resources while protecting the interests of Iberian manufacturers and merchants.

A cholera epidemic that left 30,000 dead in 1855—the largest demographic disaster to hit the island since the epidemics that decimated the Taíno population in the sixteenth century—and a series of deadly hurricanes in the 1860s embittered many on the island to the colonial government, which seemed to offer its people no respite in times of crisis and, in fact, often raised taxes in their aftermath to repair damage to fortifications and other infrastructure that provided little benefit to the workers' daily lives. At the same time, the colonial government had not invested islanders' tax money into infrastructure that might have helped to develop the local economy, areas like education, roadways, or reliable postal service.

Following the decline of the sugar market and the political and social unrest this dramatic shift sparked, the coffee industry and, to a lesser degree, the tobacco industry grew during the final three decades of the 1800s, becoming important export crops. The growth of the coffee industry and the tobacco industry (which included cigarette and cigar manufacturing) helped to develop parts of the island that had previously been sparsely inhabited by Taíno-Carib and other subsistence farmers. The southwest and interior of the island saw the development of a number of municipalities during the expansion of these two industries.

Despite these two small areas of economic growth, by the late 1860s no more than 30 percent of Puerto Rican households were characterized as "solvent," while nearly 70 percent were poor and illiteracy ran as high as 90 percent; even colonial officials described the bulk of the population as inadequately fed and clothed. Given these conditions, discontent was brewing among nearly every segment of society toward the wealthy *peninsulare* landowners and the colonial government officials who protected their interests.

EL GRITO DE LARES, 1868

In 1865 a group of liberal monarchists came to power in Spain and invited Puerto Rican colonists to participate in a fact-finding conference in Madrid. Meanwhile, back in Puerto Rico, Governor José María Marchesi thwarted a mutiny among militia members of a barracks in San Juan in June 1867. Marchesi, who opposed extending reforms to the islanders, used the mutiny to argue for tougher restrictions on the *criollos* and to undermine the reformist intentions of officials in Madrid. To underscore his argument he arrested several prominent *criollo* civilian liberals, charged them with planning the mutiny, and had them exiled.

Among the exiled *criollos* was Dr. Ramón E. Betances, a leading abolitionist and the most prominent figure in the nineteenth-century independence movement. Betances, who was exiled in 1859 for his abolitionist activities, was ordered to Madrid, but instead he and fellow revolutionary Segundo Ruiz Belvis escaped to Santo Domingo and then to New York City, where they joined members of the Republican Society of Cuba and Puerto Rico. Angered by Spanish demands for increased tax revenue to cover war expenses and public debt, Betances issued several proclamations from New York City outlining Spain's history of oppression against the *criollos* of Puerto Rico and demanding human rights for its residents. His most famous proclamation was the "Ten Commandments of Free Men," which consisted of (1) the abolition of slavery, (2) the right to vote on proposed taxes, (3) freedom of worship, (4) freedom of speech, (5) freedom of the press, (6) free trade, (7) freedom of assembly, (8) the right to bear arms, (9) inviolable citizenship, and (10) the right to elected representation. If these conditions were not granted by one's sovereign government, Betances argued, it was the right of the people to take up arms against that government and declare themselves an independent nation.

The committee and his fellow revolutionaries did not wait for a response from Spain before planning uprisings on both islands with Puerto Rico striking first. After establishing the preliminary plans and securing financial backing from sympathetic parties in the United States, Betances returned to Santo Domingo in September 1867 to plan the revolution. There he joined Ruiz Belvis and two other prominent liberal exiles to form the

Revolutionary Committee of Puerto Rico. The committee drafted a constitution on January 10, 1868, and, after secretly consulting with rebel leaders located in Puerto Rico, decided the revolution should start in the city of Camuy on September 29, 1867. However, on September 20, before the original plan could take place, the colonial government was informed of the planned insurrection and one of the organizers was arrested. Undeterred, the remaining organizers, led by Manuel Rojas of Lares, decided to move up the date of the first attack to September 23 in the city of Lares.

By early evening of September 23 about 600 men had gathered at Rojas' estate where he delivered a speech designed to stir up the revolutionary troops, promising that under a republican government taxes would be eliminated, debts canceled, and the *libreta* system ended. To demonstrate his point, he urged the *jornaleros* present to burn their passbooks; hundreds were burned on the spot. After setting the passbook bonfire, the men marched behind Rojas in two rows toward the town of Lares chanting such slogans as "Death to Spain," "Long Live Liberty," "Long Live Free Puerto Rico," and "Liberty or Death." Along the way they confronted prominent *peninsulares* and ransacked their stores. Merchants and their clerks were taken prisoner, their horses and weapons seized.

In Lares, the rebels arrested the mayor and other municipal officials, occupied City Hall, removed a portrait of the queen, declared Puerto Rico a free republic, and placed the flag of the Republic in places of prominence. From midnight to dawn they set up a provisional government, appointing rebels in their midst as officials. They declared that Spaniards living on the island had three days to declare their support of the Republic or leave.

The next day the rebels sought a priest and had him perform a blessing on the rebel troops and the new Republic, a delay that cost them valuable hours of darkness before their next attack. By the time they reached the town of Pepino it was daylight and the element of surprise could not be used to help capture the town. In addition, the mayor of Pepino had extra time to prepare for the attack he knew was coming and had asked the military commander at Aguadilla to send troops to aid in confronting the rebels. He also secured the militia's armory, a planned target of the rebels. As a result of the mayor's precautions, the rebels failed in their repeated attempts to capture the town square of Pepino. Rojas ordered his men to retreat and led them into the mountains, where he hoped they would be able to hide until Betances' scheduled attack by sea on September 29. However, word of the uprising had reached Dutch officials in St. Thomas who had seized Betances' war ship and all its equipment. Though Betances was able to escape arrest, he was not able to deliver the equipment the rebels needed to fend off government officials who had pursued them into the mountains. The government quickly rounded up some 550 rebels, ending what came to be known as El Grito de Lares (translated as the "cry" or sometimes "scream" of Lares).

Of those 550 rebels, over 90 percent had been born in Puerto Rico. This was significant because the colonial government and many historians tended to describe the Grito de Lares as a small uprising spurred by outside radicals rather than a nationalist movement of genuinely impassioned Puerto Ricans. They were also proportionally more educated and wealthier than the general population.

Initially, the colonial government sought death penalties for the most prominent rebel leaders and kept the others in crowded jail cells for so long that 80 died of yellow fever and other illnesses while waiting for trial. Fearful of popularizing the rebels' cause by creating sympathy, the Spanish authorities removed Governor Julian Juan Pavia from office, commuted the death sentences of the leaders to short prison terms, and freed nearly all the other remaining prisoners in a general amnesty. Once again, the island was awarded provincial status and citizenship was extended to *criollos*.

With Cuba now fully in the midst of a revolution, Spain could not afford to lose Puerto Rico. In the end the Grito de Lares sparked a brief period of reform by Spain's new liberal government, which had deposed Queen Isabel several days after the Grito uprising. Spain could not afford to lose its strategic gateway to the Caribbean and her leaders were willing to compromise to keep Puerto Rico under Spanish rule. In addition, it is likely that Spain's conciliatory stance following the Lares uprising was influenced by a half-century of successfully staged revolutions that had cost it nearly all its other colonies. In addition, the Lares rebellion fell between two tumultuous events for Spain: the latest overthrow of the Bourbon monarchy on September 17 and the outbreak of the first Cuban revolution, the Ten Years War, on October 10. The failure of El Grito de Lares has been attributed to Puerto Rico's lack of a well-developed *criollo* elite. In contrast to other colonies in the region, Puerto Rico's impoverished populace lacked the well-trained military leaders and well-educated statesmen and orators who had inspired successful revolts throughout nineteenth century Latin America, or even leaders with the access to sufficient resources to arm a revolutionary army and the expertise to plan for a prolonged, sustainable conflict like the Ten Years War.

It was at this point in Puerto Rico's history that a schism began to form between liberals willing to work with the ever-changing government of Spain to find some form of compromise that would put the island on the road to autonomy, and the separatists and revolutionaries for whom a free and independent Puerto Rican nation was the only solution.

So far, the independence movement's height is still the 1868 Grito de Lares. This relatively minor skirmish still has enormous symbolic importance for Puerto Ricans because it was the only significant armed uprising to ever occur on the island. Today, there are rallies, celebrations, and pro-independence demonstrations held in the central square of Lares on September 23, the anniversary of the uprising.

SLAVE REVOLTS AND ABOLITION, 1800–1873

More African slaves were brought to Puerto Rico between 1800 and 1873 than in the three previous centuries combined. Nearly 50,000 slaves entered Puerto Rico during the first half of the nineteenth century. These new African slaves were mostly children and adolescents stolen from such tribes and nations as Dahomey, Ghana, Togo, Yorubas, Wolofs, Angola, Carabilis, Igbo, modern-day Nigeria and Congo. This increase in slave traffic took place despite the fact that Spain had signed a treaty with Britain effective in 1820 promising to end the trans-Atlantic slave trade. In theory this meant that plantation owners had to be satisfied with the slaves they already owned and that any increase in their numbers could only come from births. In fact, during the 17 years that followed the agreement, more slaves than ever before were transported to Puerto Rico. Working with smugglers, the Spanish colonists essentially ignored their agreement with England. During this period slave traders began selling younger and younger slaves to Puerto Rican landowners. This new generation of adolescent and child slaves was feared by *peninsulare* landowners because newly arrived slaves were considered more likely to revolt than those who had been born into slavery.

Despite the increased importation of slaves during the sugar industry boom, the proportion of slaves to free citizens in Puerto Rico remained the smallest in the Caribbean, at just over 5 percent of the total population. However, in sugar-producing municipalities like Ponce, the second largest city on the island, the percentage approached 30 percent. It has long been argued that slavery made up an inconsequential contribution to the island's economy. Unlike its neighbors, Puerto Rico was not reliant on slave labor and Puerto Rican landowners did not treat their slaves as brutally as slave owners did elsewhere in the Americas. Traditionally, historians had maintained that the island's small proportion of slaves to wage earners and its supposedly more racially tolerant culture had prevented the slave revolts seen in other Caribbean colonial cultures. However, contemporary Afro-Puerto Rican scholars with access to previously unavailable primary documents from the Spanish colonial era have proven these long-held assertions to be false. Export industries, particularly the sugar industry, were almost entirely reliant on slave labor and landowners argued as much whenever Spanish officials considered emancipation. According to these landowners'

reports, free laborers worked only a few days a year during the plantations' busiest production periods. Of course, it is possible that the landowners were downplaying the role that free wage earners played in their
industries to maintain an essentially free labor supply. Nevertheless, there
is ample primary evidence to support the argument that the rapid economic growth experienced by Puerto Rico in the nineteenth century owed
a significant debt to the labors of its slave population.

As for the long-held argument that slaves were better treated in Puerto
Rico because they worked side-by-side with free laborers, this, too, has
been placed into question by the documentary evidence that has been
uncovered by historians specializing in Afro-Puerto Rican studies. In years
past, the lack of planned slave revolts was often cited as evidence that the
lives of Puerto Rico's slaves were not as harsh as those on other islands. In
fact, there were more than 40 planned revolts between 1795 and 1873,
according to colonial records, and many more thwarted escapes, as well as
attacks on slave owners and plantation overseers. Inspired by the successful slave revolution in Haiti, as well as revolts in Saint Lucia, Venezuela,
and other nearby colonies, slaves in Aguadilla attempted to stage a revolt
in 1795.

In 1812 a misunderstanding led to a riot in San Juan. During the Cortes
of 1812, Puerto Rican delegate Ramón Power y Giralt wrote a letter to his
mother telling her of two proposals before parliament, one that would free
newly born children of slaves and another that would end the slave trade
and free all slaves. Power y Giralt urged his mother to free her slaves immediately if either proposal was passed. After reading the letter out loud
Doña Josefa Giralt burst into tears and tore the letter to pieces. Two slaves,
Jacinto and Fermin, had seen and heard the incident and misunderstood.
Believing they were legally free, they ran away from Doña Giralt's home
and spread word among the slaves of several local haciendas that Spain
had abolished slavery throughout the empire but that the Puerto Rican
slave owners were ignoring the decree. Word quickly spread to several
municipalities, including the capital, where an uprising was planned during annual Christmas festivities. After a doubtful slave heard the news of
the abolition and the planned uprising, he told his owner and several of
the revolt's organizers were arrested. In the days that followed the rumor
continued to spread as did plans for revolt, and additional arrests were
made.

In 1821, an elaborate slave revolt was planned in Bayamón. Similar in
outline to several conspiracies that would be discovered and thwarted during the following decades, the plan called for slaves from several haciendas
to meet at a designated time to collect weapons that would be hidden in a
cane field. The armed slaves would then proceed to the nearest municipal

armory where they would take over the cache of weapons. Weapons would be distributed to slaves throughout the district and the conspiracy would culminate in the murder of all whites and the declaration of a black republic similar to the Republic of Hati. Five days before the planned revolt was set to begin one of the slaves told his master. Within days, 61 slaves from dozens of haciendas were arrested.

After a similar scheme was uncovered in Ponce in 1826 Governor de la Torre issued the island's second *Reglamento de Esclavos* (Slave Regulations), which allowed owners to use harsh punishments to prevent uprisings. The previous *Reglamento de Esclavos* of 1789 was aimed at outlining slave owners' responsibilities toward their slaves, limiting cruel treatment, and setting up a system by which slaves could earn money to buy their freedom. The difference in the two laws can be explained by the increased anxiety that the Caribbean slave revolutions had created in the white population.

Another planned revolt nearly succeeded in the town of Toa Baja in 1843 when slaves who were members of the Longoba nation escaped and captured the town munitions store. When the small band of slaves made their way to a bell tower, where it is believed that they would have sounded the alarm that would begin a more general uprising, they encountered resistance and before they could ring the bell, a band of trained militia arrived along with local volunteers. Five soldiers and at least one slave were killed in the bell tower skirmish before the slaves were forced to retreat to nearby cane fields. After the slaves were captured in the cane fields by use of fire and firearms, arrests were made and eight of the conspirators were executed.

Planned revolts increased during the 1840s, though nearly all were prevented by disclosure by informants to their owners prior to planned start dates. White residents, cognizant of the violent slave revolts that had taken place in other Caribbean colonies, pushed the colonial government for assurances that rebellions would be kept in check. In response, Governor Juan Prim issued the 1848 *Banda Contra la Raza Africana* (more commonly referred to as the Black Code). These regulations are a stunning departure from the policy of previous centuries in that they target free blacks and *mulatos* as well as slaves. The code stated that any person of the African race would be assumed to be in the wrong if they perpetrated an act of violence against a white person, even if they had been provoked or were acting to defend themselves, that all members of the black race—free or slave—were under the jurisdiction of the military, and that slave owners had the power of life and death over their slaves. The code urged owners to be vigilant in monitoring slaves' activities and outlined penalties for slave owners in the event of revolt, claiming that owners would be held financially responsible for any damage done by their slaves' activities. Such provisions led to increased corporal punishment of slaves and harsh penalties for small infractions. The code also encouraged slave owners to lock their slaves in their quarters for the night and outlawed many slave social rituals, such as *bombas* (dances), which had been a regular feature of both slave and free black culture on the island for centuries. These harsh measures provoked a slave revolt a few months after they were announced.

In addition to instituting harsh measures on slaves, the colonial government also refused to tolerate abolitionist lobbying or rhetoric from the free population, and in 1859, Governor Fernando Cotoner ordered physicians José Francisco Basora and Ramón E. Betances (more famous for his role in El Grito de Lares than for his earlier work as an abolitionist) exiled for planning to found an abolitionist society. Betances, who was of African ancestry, was well-known for saving the lives of perhaps hundreds of slaves during the cholera outbreak of 1855. But the colonial government could not silence calls for abolition and in 1864 Puerto Rican Julio L. Vizcarrondo founded an abolitionist group in Spain.

Aside from famous figures like Betances, very little is known about the free Afro-Puerto Rican population during this period of escalating slave activity. Afro-Puerto Rican scholars have had an easier time uncovering the culture of the slave community because there are more documents about this population available for study than there are documents testifying to the lives of free Puerto Rican blacks, many of whom could not write and therefore left behind few journals or letters to mine for historic or sociological data. Court documents in sugar-producing areas like Ponce, where there were large concentrations of both African slaves and free Afro-Puerto Ricans, seem to indicate that the island's racial atmosphere became increasing strained throughout the 1800s. Whiteness, these court documents seem to indicate, was increasingly equated with decency and honesty, while those of African ancestry or *mulato* status were assumed to embody opposite traits.[3] Contemporary scholars specializing in Afro-Puerto Rican history have argued that race took on greater significance following the race wars in neighboring colonies. The precarious economic backdrop and the fear created by rumors of race wars on surrounding islands certainly must have contributed to increasingly repressive social stratification based on race.

By 1869 over 50 percent of the island's population classified itself as white, about 40 percent as free persons of color, and 6.5 percent as slave. Previous census numbers over the centuries had recorded white as the minority race. It is unclear whether the census numbers reflect an actual increase in the number of white settlers to the island due to the *Cédula* de Gracias, or, as some historians have argued, a growing tendency for light-skinned Puerto Ricans to claim "white" status as race-based divisions on the island grew due to immigration from European ethnic groups with less tolerance for interracial marriage and from the race-based labor segmentation that characterized the sugar plantation economy. In fact, many contemporary Afro-Puerto Rican historians routinely use the phrase "apparently white" to describe light-skinned landowners and social actors, since these scholars maintain that, aside from newly arrived European immigrants, very few Puerto Ricans were likely to have been white. Instead, they argue, most Puerto Ricans identifying as white were in fact light-skinned *mulatos, mestizos*, or descendents of black, white, *and* Taíno-Carib bloodlines. Though Spanish-speakers across Latin America have long used a seemingly endless variety of words to describe various skin tones and variations of ethnicity, this tendency seems to have taken on an uglier connotation during this period as whiteness came to embody status, purity, and moral standing. Records from civil and criminal court cases conducted during this time period make clear what the official historians have long worked to obscure—racial relations among Puerto Ricans were not always free of tensions and injustices.

After the 1868 Grito de Lares, Spain's new liberal government invited Puerto Rico to send delegates to Madrid for another Cortes that would consider several issues affecting the island, among them abolition. Although the liberal Puerto Rican delegates argued for immediate abolition, many of the Spanish delegates wanted to move more slowly and came up with a compromise measure, the Moret Law, named for the delegate who proposed it, which would emancipate slave children and slaves older than 60. Following the Cortes, a series of liberal governors set up Puerto Rico's first elected legislative body, the Provincial Deputation, in 1870 and authorized the island's first sanctioned political parties, the Liberal Reform Party and the Conservative Party.

On March 22, 1873, Spain's Republican government abolished slavery in Puerto Rico. However, the pro-slavery movement, led in part by Puerto Rico's former governor José Laureano Sanz y Posse, added a provision to the decree that required the island's 30,000 slaves to undertake a three-year apprenticeship. The emancipation decree consisted of eight provisions: three outlining the rights of the newly liberated slaves and five protecting the rights of slave owners.

In theory, the slaves had the freedom to change employers but not their work designations. In practice few slaves had the capacity to change employers and few employers negotiated fair wages with workers they still saw as property, despite the fact that the slave owners were compensated with stipends for the loss of each slave. Three months later, in June 1873, Governor Rafael Primo de Rivera abolished the *libreta* system, which at least prevented newly released slaves from exchanging one form of endless servitude for another.

THE PATH TOWARD AUTONOMY, 1880–1898

In 1874, shortly after slavery and the *libreta* system were abolished, the Bourbon monarchs regained their seat in Spain and royalists began to erode the freedoms Puerto Ricans were just beginning to exercise. Isabel II's son, Alfonso XII, appointed a series of hard-line governors, beginning with the return of former governor and pro-slavery, anti-*criollo* stalwart José Lorenzo Sanz, who immediately began replacing elected members of the legislature with his own appointees. He fired the few *criollo* public servants on the island and replaced them with *peninsulares*. Sanz believed that the schools were responsible for fomenting discontent among the middle and working classes, so he fired all the teachers and shut down educational institutions across the island. This move forced elites to send their sons to schools in Europe and the United States, where wealthy *criollos* had a chance to see first-hand the prosperity made possible by free markets and more liberal education and social systems. Frustrated with what they were beginning to see as the forced backwardness of their homeland, many *criollos* returned to their island more determined than ever to attain independence. Still others hoped to convince Spain that Puerto Rico should become an economically autonomous Spanish territory, similar to the relationship Canada enjoyed with Great Britain. At the same time the independence movement, particularly among radical *criollos* living in New York City, was gaining supporters. It was there, in 1895, that members of the Puerto Rico Section of the Cuban Revolutionary Party created what we think of today as the Puerto Rican flag.

Members of the Liberal Reform Party (LFP) met in Ponce in 1887 to reconsider their approach. There a new party emerged; the Partido Autonomista Puertorriqueño (PAP) was established from the ruins of the LFP. Later that year, the PAP faced a reformed Conservative Party, now calling itself the Unconditionally Spanish Party (*Partido Español Sin Condiciones*, also called the *Incondicionales*, or Unconditionals in English). When it appeared that the PAP would prevail in the coming elections, the Unconditionals turned to violence, attacking PAP candidates and destroying their property. In response the PAP organized a boycott of Spanish-owned businesses. In addition, *peninsulare* stores were robbed and damaged, though the PAP denied responsibility and even claimed that the Unconditionals had staged the vandalism. Eventually the new governor, Romualdo Palacio ordered the arrest and torture of 80 PAP members. Alarmed, government officials in Madrid quickly removed Palacio from office. Violent outbreaks characterized local politics until the end of the century. A rift soon formed between the older members of the PAP, who still hoped to seek accommodation with the colonial government, and younger, foreign-educated members who urged a more radical stance in demanding autonomy. Representing the younger PAP members was Luis Muñoz Rivera, who preferred to circumvent local Spanish authorities and negotiate directly with Spain. Shortly afterward, the party went back to being referred to as the Liberal Party.

In 1896 Muñoz Rivera led the autonomists' commission to Spain, where he argued that reform and autonomy were the best defense against revolution. By the late 1890s, Spain was contending with frequent regime changes and almost continuous unrest at home, and conducting a war against revolutionary forces in Cuba. In light of these struggles, capitulating to the demands of Muñoz Rivera's autonomists must have seemed prudent. In 1897 Spain granted the island a limited autonomy. It would be governed by a Spanish-appointed executive branch and a democratically elected legislature as well as democratically elected local city and village councils. An autonomous government was authorized on November 25, 1897. The Autonomic Charter granted Puerto Rico elected representation through a legislative body at home and in the Cortes in Spain. The governor would remain an appointed position, named by the Spanish head of state. In addition, democratically elected Puerto Ricans would have a voice in the Spanish government. The island legislature would have the right to negotiate trade terms independently with foreign powers. Perhaps most importantly, the Charter could not be amended except by request of the Puerto Rican legislature.

It was not quite independence, but it was an autonomy approaching that of Canada, the model Muñoz Rivera was seeking to emulate. Yet, no one, not even Muñoz Rivera, had expected Spain to grant this level of autonomy so soon. The news was cause for joy and pride for Puerto Ricans, but there was also skepticism. After so many years of austerity and broken promises, some thought the news too good to be true.

Muñoz Rivera's party won nearly all the available seats in the new legislature and the cabinet, with Muñoz Rivera as president, was installed in February 1898. However, the legislature's first session was postponed when the United States declared war against Spain in March 1898.

5

U.S. Territory: Military Occupation and Civil Government (1898–1948)

PRELUDE: THE HOLSTEIN CONSPIRACY

In 1822, Docoudray Holstein attempted to set up the Republic of Boricua with U.S. backing. Holstein, who was born in Alsace, Germany, fought alongside Simón Bolívar in his revolution to evict the Spanish from Latin America. After a falling out with Bolívar, Holstein settled in the Caribbean island of Curacao, and then traveled to Philadelphia, where he met exiled Cuban and Puerto Rican independence activists. He began raising money for a Puerto Rican revolution from U.S. merchants in Philadelphia, New York, Boston, and New Jersey. Holstein's backers thought an independent Puerto Rico would open up revenue opportunities that would not exist as long as the island remained a Spanish colony. In addition to raising funds for weapons and other equipment, Holstein also attracted as many as 500 adventurers to his cause, all of whom were ready to journey to the Caribbean to depose the Spanish. Several national newspapers also backed Holstein's plan, which called for the revolutionaries to leave from several ports on the same day and converge on the island. Once there, Holstein and his adventurers thought they could count on the island's slaves to revolt and join the revolution and depose the Spanish. News of the plot reached Spanish authorities while Holstein's ships were in transit, and Spanish troops were mobilized along the island's shores and ports. News of the revolutionary expedition also seems to have reached slave communities throughout Puerto Rico, because Spanish authorities squelched a series of simultaneous revolts on October 12, 1822, around the time that Holstein's attack was expected. The slave revolts were prevented and Holstein's band of liberators never reached Puerto Rico. His schooner ran off course and took on water, forcing him to land in his old home base of Curacao, where he was arrested by Dutch authorities.

The Holstein Conspiracy was not the only example of businessmen, journalists, and other powerful entities in U.S. society expressing interest in liberating and/or occupying Puerto Rico and other European-controlled islands in the Caribbean. Several U.S. presidents offered to purchase Cuba and/or Puerto Rico from Spain at various points during the eighteenth and nineteenth centuries. Official U.S. policy, from the 1820s through 1850, was not to expend military resources on acquiring Cuba or Puerto Rico as long as they remained in Spanish hands. Spain was a crumbling empire and posed little threat to the southern United States. What the U.S. government most hoped to prevent was the acquisition of Cuba or Puerto Rico by a stronger European power such as England or France. In fact, Simón Bolívar intended to expand his revolutionary activities to Cuba and Puerto Rico, but he amended his plans when he learned that the United States did not desire the islands' independence from Spain.

Interest in Cuba, and to a lesser degree Puerto Rico, intensified after the 1845 annexation of Texas and the 1848 land acquisitions that resulted from the U.S. victory in the Mexican-American War. As a result of that war the United States had acquired a taste for expansionism, which it articulated as Manifest Destiny, a policy based on the belief that the United States was destined to control an increasing swath of the Americas, with God's blessing. In more practical terms, expansionists believed the U.S. economy would be strengthened by access to resources, markets, and labor sources in Latin America and the Pacific. Cuba was especially prized because militarists argued that it might someday be needed to help defend Florida. Its occupation by a strong European power, such as England or France, would pose a threat to the territorial integrity of the southern United States. Some proponents of Manifest Destiny believed that the United States should control all of the Caribbean and North America.

By the end of the nineteenth century, expansionist journalists, business leaders, and politicians called on the government to assist Cuban nationalists in their revolution against Spain. The rhetoric of these calls to war focused on Spain's tyranny over the Cuban people, but the motivations to forge a strong alliance with a free Cuba (or to replace Spain as an occupying power) were financial and military. Though most proponents of intervention in Cuba were not advocating the liberation of Puerto Rico, a few key players, such as then-Assistant Secretary of the Navy Theodore Roosevelt, secretly urged President William McKinley to include Puerto Rico in any eventual war plans.

SPANISH-AMERICAN WAR

In 1895 both Cuba and the Philippines revolted against Spain. For Cuba this was a re-ignition of its 1868 to 1878 revolution. Pro-expansionist newspapers in the United States, particularly the Hearst syndicate, made the events of the war in Cuba front-page news, highlighting perceived brutality by the Spanish troops against the Cuban revolutionaries with banner headlines and lurid illustrations. It did not help matters for the Spanish when its top general in Cuba, Valeriano Weyler y Nicolau, began interring the civilian population in camps to keep them from joining the revolutionaries. Poor sanitation and inadequate housing and food supplies in the camps caused illness and starvation among families and children. It has been estimated that as many as 100,000 people died in the camps. U.S. citizens who read in the newspapers about the suffering of those residing in the camps were outraged and called on the U.S. government to do something to end it. On entering office in March 1897, President William McKinley demanded that Spain end the internment policy and relinquish its control over Cuba. Spain refused.

The war between the United States and Spain was finally triggered by the sinking of the *Maine*, a U.S. battleship that had been sent to Havana Harbor in January 1898. On February 15, 1898, the *Maine* blew up and its 266 crewmembers were killed. Many U.S. historians and nearly all Puerto Rican and Latin American historians now maintain that the sinking of the *Maine* was staged by the U.S. government as an excuse to start the war in the hopes of gaining territory in the Caribbean. Others have hypothesized that mechanical error was responsible for sinking the ship. Following the incident, a U.S. investigation declared that it had been blown up by a mine, although a Spanish investigation suggested mechanical error. The U.S. press, led by the Hearst syndicate, blamed the tragedy on sabotage by the Spanish and public opinion began to mount in favor of an invasion of Cuba.

On April 19, 1898, Congress granted President William McKinley authority to use military force to expel the Spanish from Cuba. At the same time, U.S. Senator Henry Teller proposed an amendment to the military authorization that precluded the United States retaining Cuba as a colony.

In response, Spain declared war on the United States and the United States declared war on Spain on April 25. The declaration of war opened the battlefield beyond Cuba, allowing U.S. expansionists to cast their net on Spain's other remaining colonies, the Philippines and Puerto Rico. And there was nothing like the Teller Amendment standing in the way of making colonies of either the Philippines or Puerto Rico.

By the end of the nineteenth century, Spain, once the largest empire in the world due to its fifteenth-century discoveries in the Americas, was a collapsing remnant of the world power it had once been. Its population of 18 million was dwarfed by the United States with its growing populace of 75 million. Spain's economy was contracting, while the U.S. economy was growing exponentially. Spain's one advantage was its military, which consisted of over 300,000 men, many of them already deployed in Cuba, Puerto Rico, and the Philippines. The United States had a 28,000-man Army and about 114,000 additional men who could be called on from state militias. This problem was largely solved by the war's popularity. Volunteers lined up to oust the Spanish from Cuba. In part a younger generation hoped to capture some of the glory that the Civil War generation still held in the popular imagination. By the end of the summer the Army had almost 300,000 men in uniform. In addition, the United States hoped to rely on its stronger navy to win the war with blockades of Cuba and Puerto Rico's harbors that would prevent Spain from deploying its Iberian-based troops.

The U.S. war effort was speedily planned, and the new recruits barely trained and inadequately supplied. Spain, however, was not able to take advantage of these weaknesses. On all three fronts—Cuba, Puerto Rico, and the Philippines—Spanish resistance was disorganized and U.S. victory swift.

In Cuba and Puerto Rico, the United States chose similar strategies. After rejecting initial plans to bombard and attack the capitals of each island, it was decided that the navy would bombard the islands from various harbors, initiate ground force attacks in key cities where they suspected that Spanish defenses were weakest, and gradually work toward capturing the colonial capitals of Havana and San Juan. On both fronts victory occurred more swiftly than had been anticipated.

General Nelson Miles, the highest-ranking U.S. officer in the Caribbean, arrived in Cuba just as the Spanish were surrendering. He left Cuba July 21 with six ships and 3,400 men heading for Puerto Rico where he expected to face Spanish forces of about 9,000. Nearly 15,000 more U.S. troops were on their way from training facilities in Tampa, Florida, and Charleston, South Carolina.

Meanwhile, in Puerto Rico, the U.S. Navy had started bombarding the fortifications of San Juan from sea on May 12. On July 25, 1898, General Miles and his troops came ashore near the town of Guánica on the southwestern coast. U.S. troops encountered almost no resistance. In the following days troops landed in Ponce and Arroyo. The Spanish troops under the leadership of the governor, General Manuel Macías y Casado, were positioned to meet the U.S. invaders at San Juan, Ponce, Mayaguez, and Caguas. Macías accurately realized that he was outnumbered two-to-one and that he could not count on support from the native-born population who favored the U.S. troops.

Given Puerto Rico's history of native resistance to outside invasion, U.S. forces had been trained to expect and were prepared to encounter resistance from the criollos, famed for fending off English and Dutch invaders in earlier centuries. Instead, they were welcomed. Records from the time show that many Puerto Ricans were dubious that Spain truly intended to grant the autonomy they had been promised in 1897. The Puerto Rican people, who admired the United States for overthrowing Britain's colonial rule and for gaining prominence and economic independence from Europe, thought that the United States was more likely to allow them sovereignty and that the transition would be more orderly than it might have been under Spain. The people of Puerto Rico felt assured that their island would be granted independence or eventually become a state, and that either of these possibilities would ensure greater prosperity and liberty. U.S. troops were greeted in most parts of the island as liberators.

For the first time in 400 years the local Puerto Rican population did not come to the defense of the Spanish authority when faced with a foreign invader. In fact, many Puerto Ricans actively helped the U.S. forces, serving as guides, suppliers, interpreters, and mule drivers. With an enemy outmanned two-to-one and a native population that was actively helping the invasion force, General Macías relayed his assessment of the situation to Madrid: The Spanish had no hope of victory.

The military campaign lasted 19 days, during which seven U.S. soldiers, 34 Spanish troops, and eight Spanish civilians were killed. An armistice was announced August 12 and the Treaty of Paris signed on December 10, 1898.

Before the short war had ended the expansionist McKinley administration decided it would attempt to annex Puerto Rico and negotiate control of the island during peace talks. Throughout the treaty negotiations, the United States maintained that control over Puerto Rico and the Philippines was owed as fair compensation for the cost of the war. In its final form, the treaty forced Spain to evacuate Cuba, which the United States promised not to incorporate as a territory, and to cede to the United States Puerto Rico, the Philippines, and Guam. Article 9 of the treaty stated that, "The civil rights and political status of the native inhabitants hereby ceded to the United States shall be determined by the Congress," while the tenth article guaranteed the residents of the ceded territories freedom of religion, their only enumerated right.

Puerto Rican members of the New York-based Cuban Revolutionary Party felt betrayed. Cuba, it seemed, would gain its freedom, thanks to the Teller Amendment, but there would no such guarantees for Puerto Rico.

Some Puerto Rican politicians and historians have argued that the Treaty of Paris is an unlawful document because Spain had signed the Autonomic Charter Puerto Rico in 1897 and, therefore, Spain did not have the right to give an island it no longer controlled, but only helped to govern by mutual consent, to another nation. Others argue that since the Charter did not actually grant Puerto Rico independence, but rather a limited form of local self-rule, the Spanish did not violate the spirit of the Autonomic Charter in signing the Treaty of Paris with the United States. What is clear is that the United States did not consider itself bound by the Charter, which granted Puerto Rico more autonomy than it enjoys in its relationship with the United States to this day.

U.S. MILITARY OCCUPATION (OCTOBER 1898–MAY 1900)

When the United States invaded in 1898, the island's population was over 1 million and had increased six-fold during the nineteenth century. Most of these 1 million inhabitants were living as wage laborers or subsistence farmers and an increasing proportion of the island's land was owned by a small number of families in the sugar, coffee, and tobacco industries. Though 85 percent of the population lived in rural areas, most of the country's food was imported. This dependence on food transported from abroad meant that during times of economic crisis or following natural disasters, such as hurricanes, many of the rural poor went hungry. Their dwellings were rudimentary, with water, cooking, and bathroom facilities outside the home. Health care was provided by *curanderos*, or healers, whose herbal remedies could do little in the face of illnesses created by malnutrition and the hygiene problems inherent to industrialized agriculture. Clothing was inadequate to protect the poor against the elements and three out of four Puerto Ricans had never worn shoes.[1]

This portrait of life before the arrival of U.S. forces on Puerto Rico's shores does not correspond to the pastoral paradise that members of the New York-based independence movement would try to perpetuate in the 1920s. Many historians and political activists have described the island prior to U.S. domination as prosperous, populated by a well-educated harmonious multicultural agrarian society. Ironically, many Puerto Ricans who offered no resistance to the U.S. invasion seemed to have visions of Puerto Rico under U.S. control that weren't far off from this same idyllic picture. As detailed in previous chapters, Puerto Rico's years under Spanish rule were far from idyllic, filled with tensions and challenges. Its years as a U.S. territory (under U.S. Constitutional definitions it is technically an unincorporated territory) would prove just as challenging.

Puerto Ricans were already familiar with the United States through its consumer and cultural products. Puerto Ricans were quick to adopt baseball in the late nineteenth century and the dollar had been used as currency there for some time. The United States was perceived as the origin of liberty and independence from corrupt European rule, and Puerto Ricans felt sure that once the U.S. military had safely delivered them from the Spanish, the U.S. government would right all the injustices on the island, leaving Puerto Rico as an independent nation or perhaps on the road to statehood.

Immediately after the U.S. invasion there were a series of demonstrations held demanding that the hacienda owners leave the island. These rallies were likely caused by the widely held belief that the Americans were going to free up the land previously owned by the Spanish *peninsulares* and redistribute it to the workers. Although everyday Puerto Ricans were familiar with George Washington the revolutionary, they were less familiar with George Washington the businessman and slave owner.

U.S. perceptions of Puerto Rico were wildly inaccurate as well. Many thought that it was located in the China Sea, while others thought that it was attached to Cuba. A book of photographs published in 1899 titled *Our Island and Their People* depicting the island's quaint poverty and agrarian lifeways in words and pictures couldn't have stated the paternalistic approach the U.S. government would take in more stark terms. As far as the U.S. expansionists were concerned, the island belonged to "us" and the people who happened to live there were "they," "other," foreign, and passive.

Just prior to the invasion, the island had experienced a prolonged drought, followed by the blockade and, during the ground force invasion, flooding. What little food was still grown on the island had been nearly impossible to harvest and the food that ordinarily would have been imported from the United States was delayed by the war. In desperation, bands of armed young men began traveling the countryside just after the Spanish withdrew, raiding food and other materials from wealthy Spanish families and merchants.

The bands became increasingly violent as the weeks and months passed and conditions failed to improve. They no longer restricted their raids to haciendas owned by Spanish families, for example, and began targeting wealthy native-born families as well. Sometimes they burned down homes and other buildings. There were even instances of beatings or murders of hacienda owners. In addition to theft, vandalism, and occasional violence, the bands of raiders also used the opportunity to destroy records of debts kept in hacienda stores. Under Spanish law wageworkers could not seek new employment or better wages until all debts had been paid to their current employer. This system meant that most of Puerto Rico's rural poor lived as debt-indentured near-slaves, unable to seek a better paying job or move to another area of the country until all their debts were paid. Since imported food and other goods often cost more than wages earned, many laborers saw no way out: They would work for a single employer their whole lives and die in debt. In this light, it is easy to see how the bands' destruction of the debt records was cheered by their neighbors.

The U.S. military government, inexperienced at occupation, was ill-equipped to effectively deal with this humanitarian crisis. What was needed was a massive logistical effort to feed the people of Puerto Rico. Instead, military leaders concentrated their efforts on capturing the "bandits." Because U.S. military leaders perceived the crisis through their own cultural lens, they casted the band members as criminals, disturbing the peace and threatening vulnerable law-abiding citizens, à la the Old West of the American frontier. In contrast, many working-class Puerto Ricans saw the bands as young men inflamed by the passions of war, attempting to exact revenge for old injustices. Others saw band members, such as legendary band leader "White Eagle," as folk heroes, the country's earliest revolutionary force, resisting U.S. occupation in its earliest stages. This gap in perception presages many of the cultural misunderstandings that would characterize Puerto Rico's modern era as a U.S. colony/commonwealth.

Politics

In their new and unaccustomed role as liberators (some would argue colonizers), U.S. military leaders adopted a paternalistic role, allowing local leaders even less say in the governance of their island than they had enjoyed in Puerto Rico's final years as a Spanish colony. Even before the Treaty of Paris was signed, the U.S. military began the process of taking over power from the local colonial administrators, which was to be expected, and from locally elected native Puerto Ricans, which was shocking and disheartening for members of the island's elite as well as for its workers.

General Miles left the island two days after the peace protocol was signed and General John R. Brooke became the island's first U.S. military governor. Brooke only held his post for a few months before becoming governor of Cuba, but during that time he made his lack of respect for the elected leaders and institutions of the island clear. Ignoring orders to retain as much of the existing governmental institutions and processes as possible, he suppressed the legislative body and made changes to the judicial system. During September and October, his troops traveled from town to town, installing officers in place of the local mayors, and hoisting the U.S. flag in place of the Spanish flag, until the Stars and Stripes was finally hoisted in San Juan on October 18, 1898.

After Brooke's departure, Major General Guy Henry was installed as governor. As these changes took place, the democratically elected cabinet, led by the pro-autonomist Liberal Party, tried to carry on, but was soon disbanded by General Henry, who appointed his own cabinet. In February 1899, the governor disbanded the Insular Council, the last remaining institution from the period of Autonomy. Treating the island like an army base, the military officers tolerated no criticism and shut down newspapers and jailed editors who dared to question these decisions. It even kept the newspapers from reporting on strikes and disturbances, creating the false impression of a perfectly peaceful transfer of power. This turn of events soured many of the island's local leaders on U.S. rule and would play a role in the relationship between Puerto Rico and the United States for years to come.

However, local leaders still attempted to make a public show of welcoming the military government. Even after being removed from elected office, leading autonomist Muñoz Rivera expressed his admiration for the United States and his faith that, after a short transition period, the most famous democracy in the world would leave the governance of Puerto Rico to Puerto Ricans.

U.S. Politics

Meanwhile in Washington, D.C., a political debate ensued over the future of Puerto Rico between expansionists on one side and those who did not favor the United States taking and holding territories by force on the other. Many in the United States believed that any territory under U.S. control had to begin steps to become a state or be allowed to become an independent sovereign nation. These were the only two options available, anti-expansionists argued. Any other possibility would be a violation of the U.S. Constitution. With these sympathies in mind, expansionist military leaders and war correspondents downplayed the part played by Puerto Ricans (and Cubans) in helping U.S. forces defeat the Spanish. U.S. troops were given full credit for the glorious resounding victory, while the Puerto Rican people were portrayed as passive bystanders indifferent to their fate. This narrative helped bolster the argument that the U.S. government did not owe the Puerto Rican people anything for the victory because they had not helped bring it about. Since the United States owed the people of Puerto Rico no political debts, it was not obligated to grant them either independence or statehood.

Most U.S. lawmakers, including the anti-expansionists, did not support statehood. The arguments against statehood were many, but racism seems to have been the most popular. Records of Congressional debate surrounding the issue of governing Puerto Rico from this era, prior to the military government's withdrawal in 1899, contain a great deal of racist rhetoric that would be considered shocking by today's standards. However, it must be remembered that these debates were taking place during an era when the Jim Crow laws were in full effect throughout the South. Puerto Ricans, according to the race-based argument against statehood, would not fit into the union. They had a different culture, history, language, and they were of a different race (there was quite a bit of argument over what exactly that race was), and would not fit into the Anglo-Saxon cultural and moral traditions of the United States. Even the island's Catholicism was cited as a mark against its possible place in the Union.

On the other hand, these same traits made the Puerto Ricans too inept to govern themselves. Though a more paternalistic tone characterized debate surrounding the possibility of granting Puerto Rico independence, racism remained an underlying element. Lawmakers argued that Puerto Ricans were not educated enough and did not have enough experience with democracy to govern themselves.

The country that had gone to war to liberate one people from the tyranny of empire, was now claiming the right to own another country with no intention of ever making it a state or an independent nation. The United States, a country established on the theory that colonization was innately unjust, was taking on the role of colonizer.

Puerto Rican Politics

Back on the island, the first two political parties that formed after the invasion were the Federalist and Republican parties, both of which favored the island's recognition as an organized U.S. territory in preparation for eventual statehood.

The leader of the first pro-statehood party, the Republicans, was José Celso Barbosa, a black doctor, who graduated from the University of Michigan in 1877. While in the United States he forged a loyalty to the U.S. Republican Party as the party of Lincoln and the abolition of slavery. Barbosa claimed that there was no "race problem" in Puerto Rico and his fervor for all things American underscored his belief that free enterprise and unfettered capitalism would allow hard-working Puerto Ricans of talent to rise to the highest ranks of society. For this reason he was not out to abolish the existing class structure. His faith in the country and the party of Lincoln meant that he was willing to wait for increased autonomy and/ or statehood until Congress deemed it appropriate. Barbosa's sincere admiration for the United States made him a perfect spokesman for the wealthy, who made up the bulk of the pro-American Republican Party membership.

The Federalists, led by Muñoz Rivera, also favored eventual statehood, after a period of autonomous government, including the right of the people to elect their own governor and enact laws not subject to overview by the

U.S. Congress. The military government saw the Federalists as a threat and threw their support behind the Republicans.

Economics

Emboldened by the U.S. invasion, many workers in 1899 refused to work for vouchers and demanded to be paid in currency. Landowners were surprised when the provisional military government occasionally backed the workers in disputes, including the voucher issue. Not only did the military leaders tell the landowners that they would have to pay the workers in currency, but they also instituted an eight-hour workday. However, on most issues the military and later the civil U.S. governments tended to side with landowners and business interests.

The sector that gained the most from the transfer from Spanish to U.S. control was the sugar industry, which almost immediately overtook coffee as the leading industry on the island. This was because the United States was the largest consumer of Puerto Rican sugar. Conversely, coffee and tobacco, which depended on European markets, suffered under the new economic conditions. The United States insisted that its commercial fleet be used to carry goods abroad, increasing costs for local sugar, coffee, and tobacco suppliers. U.S.-imposed tariffs meant that Puerto Rico could not negotiate with its former trading partners individually. A lack of ready credit for islanders, an arbitrary exchange rate that favored the dollar over the peso and diminished the net worth of all Puerto Ricans, rich and poor, literally overnight, and interest rates of up to 18 percent on loans with land as collateral made it easy for offshore business interests, particularly those from the United States, to take over much of the available property on the island. In a few short years, U.S. interests, most of them absentee corporations, owned about half the sugar-generating land. In addition, small farmers and coffee producers were hard hit by an income tax of 2 percent. The governor appointed the land assessors who often assessed the value above what the farmers could pay given the new restrictions on negotiating favorable coffee import rates with European consumers. Soon, 85 percent of coffee-producing land and 50 percent of public utilities were owned by non-Puerto Ricans. The four leading banks were U.S. and Canadian, the most powerful of which was the aptly named American Colonial Bank. Most borrowers who were deemed "qualified" by these lending institutions were from the United States. By 1930, 95 percent of Puerto Rico's trade was with the United States. The monetary policy put into place in 1898 laid the groundwork for the eventual devastation of the island's agricultural sector. It never recovered.

The shift in ownership that put a large percentage of Puerto Rico's land and industry in the hands of absentee U.S. owners was swift and left even the island's elite in a vulnerable position. Soon, some of the island's wealthiest *criollo* families were sending their sons abroad to learn how to become high-level assistants to foreign-owned manufacturers. Engineering and law degrees proliferated among the island's elite, even as they held a diminishing percentage of the island's land and capital.

Conversely, some local sugar producers managed to hold on and reap unprecedented profits in the years after the Spanish-American War. Access to new equipment helped some families in the sugar industry see record profits. These families became backers of the new regime, many of them taking part in pro-American movements and becoming active in the various incarnations of the pro-statehood political parties throughout the decades to come.

THE FORAKER ACT

In the debate leading up to the Foraker Act, Congress was persuaded by reports from the military government and others that the Puerto Ricans were not ready for self-government or even incorporated territorial status, the form of government that typically preceded statehood. Instead, in mid-1900, Congress created an unprecedented system of government no other U.S. territory had ever been subjected to, with presidential and War Department appointees holding the bulk of the power and doing the bulk of the governing, and local democratically elected officials providing extremely limited input in decision making.

When it went into effect on May 1, 1990, the Foraker Act replaced the military occupation with a government largely presided over by U.S. civilians, including a civilian governor, an 11-member executive council that would also serve as the upper house of the legislature, a 35-member lower house of the legislature (the only governmental body that would consist of democratically elected Puerto Ricans), and a supreme court. The governor, executive council, supreme court justices, and cabinet members would all be appointed by the President of the United States. In addition, any laws passed by the lower legislative body, the only segment of this governmental mechanism that was actually voted on by the people, could be vetoed by the governor, the Executive Council, or the U.S. Congress.

The provision of the Act that sparked the most anger from Puerto Rico's elite landowners and merchants was a costly tariff on goods from the island, even those heading for the United States. Not only would this provision limit commercial opportunities for sugar, coffee, and tobacco exporters, but it also made clear that the United States viewed Puerto Rico as a possession and not as an integral part of itself in the way an incorporated territory destined to become a state was legally seen. Elites were wounded by the political message inherent in the Foraker Act. Unlike Hawaii, whose path from territory to state paralleled Puerto Rico's association with the United States chronologically, Puerto Rico was not looked on by Congress as a potential state, as an entity destined to become an equal member of the United States.

Despite the islanders' disappointment, some saw hope in the Foraker Act's creation of the office of Resident Commissioner, a delegate who would speak for the interests of Puerto Ricans among government entities in Washington, D.C. However, the Foraker Act was a disappointment to most Puerto Ricans, including the pro-U.S. elite. It provided far less self-rule than had the Autonomic Charter with Spain. Legally, the Act, and particularly its tariff provision, meant that Puerto Rico was an unincorporated territory, and, in all but name, still a colony. For the governed, all that had changed was that Puerto Rico's new colonizing power did not even share its language or culture. Many Puerto Ricans expressed frustration and feelings of betrayal. They had hoped for more.

After the Foraker Act was enacted, the United States installed the island's first civilian governor, Charles Allen, and most of the U.S. troops left the island by June 1900, though several military bases remained on the island. Elections were held for the lower house of the legislature in 1900. Foraker's hated tariff provision did not last long and by 1901 free trade was established between the United States and Puerto Rico, though Congress still negotiated and set trading terms between Puerto Rico and all her other trading partners. In 1904, the status of the Resident Commissioner was upgraded to a non-voting delegate in the U.S. House of Representative, empowered to communicate the concerns of the people of Puerto Rico to Congress.

Leading autonomist and for a time Resident Commissioner Luis Muñoz Rivera continued to push the United States to grant Puerto Rico true independence. Short of that, he pushed for a plebiscite, or referendum, that would allow island residents to vote for a range of options, from independence to local self-rule under the mantle of U.S. affiliation to statehood. His Federalist party, now renamed the Union, called for the same. In his newspaper, *La Democracia*, Muñoz Rivera argued that Puerto Rico's political dignity rested on her ability to determine her own future through this democratic procedure, but he died in 1916 without seeing this dream realized.

THE JONES ACT

The Jones Act, enacted in 1916, improved some elements of Puerto Rican governance. For example, it created a legislative body in which both chambers would be elected by popular vote. Suffrage was extended to all men 21 or older. The governor, auditor, and commissioner of education remained presidential appointees, while the remaining eight members of the Executive Council, though they would be appointed by the governor, at least required the approval of the Puerto Rican Senate to assume their posts. The Jones Act also granted U.S. citizenship to all Puerto Ricans. Together the Foraker and Jones acts are sometimes referred to as the Organic Acts and provisions from each are still used as the basis for decisions rendered by courts on and off the island when making rulings on issues of governance.

Debate surrounding the extension of U.S. citizenship to all Puerto Ricans prompted yet more racist rhetoric among some members of the U.S. Congress, reminiscent of the racist rhetoric used in the Foraker Act debates to argue against Puerto Rico's incorporation as a state. Those who favored the citizenship provision argued that it would help to silence the independence movement. The independence movement and pro-labor activism were a cause for alarm for business owners in 1916, a year that saw labor strikes among many of the island's industries. That year, more than 40,000 sugar industry workers waged a strike that lasted for more than five months, while 50,000 workers held strikes to protest conditions in the tobacco industry, and dock workers participated in strikes that interrupted shipping in several port cities. Business interests in Washington, D.C., Wall Street, and San Juan hoped that granting Puerto Ricans U.S. citizenship would instill a sense of loyalty toward the United States and perhaps provide workers with the hope that their rights could be protected and their complaints could be addressed in less costly and destructive ways—at least that is what some more moderate voices in the debate argued.

At the same time, the extension of U.S. citizenship was criticized by many of Puerto Rico's political leaders, who argued that it was a way of retaining Puerto Ricans as subjects of the United States without any intention of making Puerto Rico a state. In addition, critics like Muñoz Rivera argued, U.S. citizenship would present an obstacle to eventual independence if the Puerto Rican people desired it later. Many Puerto Rican leaders, including Muñoz, said that Puerto Ricans were receiving a second-class version of U.S. citizenship because those living on the island would not be able to vote for President or for a voting delegation to the U.S. House and Senate. However, once a Puerto Rican left the island and established residency in the United States, he would be eligible to vote in local, statewide, and national elections. Some Puerto Ricans criticized this as a citizenship whose agency depended on mere geography. This situation has persisted under the island's current Commonwealth status.

Because the United States was also considering declaring war against Germany and entering World War I, some claimed that the Jones Act gave Puerto Ricans U.S. citizenship in time to draft them into military service. In fact, residents of U.S. territories do not need to be citizens to be conscripted into the military during wartime. In addition, volunteer rates for World War I and every U.S. military action that has followed have been exceptionally high among Puerto Ricans.

Despite the many objections of their leaders, everyday Puerto Ricans seemed to welcome citizenship. The law did not essentially change migration status for Puerto Ricans; however, after it was passed several thousand immediately took advantage of what they saw as the clarified migration status that U.S. citizenship created, starting new lives in the United States almost before the ink on the Act had dried.

Migration

During the 1800s a number of Puerto Rican elites traveled to the United States to attend U.S. universities, to work for U.S. firms and industries, and as exiles at odds with the Spanish colonial government. Since the 1898 U.S. invasion there had been steady migration by Puerto Ricans to the United States, especially since even without U.S. citizenship the courts had established that Puerto Ricans were free to enter the mainland at any time as residents of a U.S. territory. During World War I the government transported about 13,000 Puerto Ricans to the States to help manufacture munitions. When a large number died as a result of unsanitary conditions during transit, as well as from unsafe working conditions in the workers' camps that were hastily built to accommodate them, reforms were passed to create healthier migration conditions for Puerto Ricans, particularly those who were being transferred at the government's or an industry's expense.

Puerto Ricans began migrating in even larger numbers after the Jones Act declared them U.S. citizens. This large, continuous migration pattern helped to alleviate unemployment issues that intensified with the early twentieth century shift from an agrarian to an industrial economy, especially during the Depression. By 1920 there were 45,000 Puerto Ricans living in New York City. Many of these migrants were former agriculture workers from Puerto Rico's coffee and tobacco regions.

Arturo Schomburg

One of these early Puerto Rican New Yorkers (later to be called Nuyoricans) was Arturo A. Schomburg, who was born in San Juan in 1874 and spent part of his childhood in St. Thomas. According to legend, his legacy as one of the world's most famous collectors and archivists of African culture was cemented by the following exchange he had with one of his teachers in Puerto Rico. When the young Arturo asked why the textbook his class was reading made no mention of African culture, he was told it was because Africa had no culture. Later, as a young man, he joined a group of Puerto Rican intellectuals on a journey to collect Puerto Rican documents from an archive in Madrid. This quest may have inspired him to begin the archiving project that would become his lifelong mission. After moving to New York, he joined the African separatist movement and developed an admiration for its most famous leader, Marcus Garvey. He was also a member of the Revolutionary Committee of Puerto Rico. Schomburg's collection of books, manuscripts, and art relating to Africans and the African Diaspora was purchased by the New York Public Library's Division of Negro Literature, History, and Prints in 1926. Today, his collection is a cornerstone of Harlem's Schomburg Center for Research in Black Culture, one of the world's most important centers for research on the African Diaspora.

Culture Clash: Education

The most obvious mark of distinction between Puerto Ricans and their U.S. colonizers was language. Puerto Ricans embraced their language in a way they had not done under Spanish rule when they had shared a language with the ruling regime. This became contentious when a series of U.S. governors, as well as some pro-statehood leaders, insisted that children should be taught in English.

Following the invasion, the military government shifted the role of education from the church to the government. This was a profound cultural shift for students, families, and teachers. The U.S. military and early civilian governments set up dozens of schools, including high schools (most Puerto Rican students at the time stopped attending school after four years), and in 1903 the University of Puerto Rico.

Schools were seen as tools of Americanization. American flags were assigned to each school and children began each school day saluting the flag, saying the Pledge of Allegiance, and singing patriotic songs. Teachers were required to learn English and encouraged to teach all subjects in English. Those who failed to learn English fast enough were fired and replaced by teachers from the United States. During the earliest years of U.S. administration, nearly half of the island's teachers were sent to summer seminars at Harvard and Columbia universities, where they were taught English and U.S. teaching theories and methods. Hundreds, possibly thousands, of students were sent via government-funded scholarships to U.S. boarding schools. Some students who the government had determined met an Amerindian racial phenotype were sent to controversial Indian residential schools, whose primary mission was to "civilize" students by discouraging them from practicing their culture or using their indigenous languages.

Puerto Ricans who seemed to fit U.S. administrators' conception of an African racial phenotype were sent to segregated African American vocational boarding schools. During school breaks the boarding school students were often sent to work as servants for host families.

Finally, in 1942, after decades of failed experimentation that critics said left the majority of Puerto Rico's children illiterate in both English and Spanish, Spanish was declared the official language of instruction for all students through eighth grade in Puerto Rico's public schools.

In addition to the language debate, there were debates over school holidays. School was closed for all U.S. holidays, many of which had no meaning or context for Puerto Rican families and their children. In contrast, it took much debate before the U.S. education minister allowed the observance of Three Kings' Day, an important religious holiday throughout Latin America.

In addition to the Spanish language and religious traditions and rituals, other Puerto Rican traditions counter to U.S. culture that continued in the face of disapprobation from the military and civil government included cock fighting and the production and consumption of rum during Prohibition.

Religion

Today, about two-thirds of the population is Roman Catholic and one-third Protestant Christian. When the U.S. military government took over the school system and other social/cultural functions on the island in 1898, the population was almost entirely Catholic and the church was a central part of most people's lives. Schools were run by the church and civic celebrations were held on religious holidays and the feast days of the saints. Attempts to separate church and state and to limit the number of religious holidays celebrated by the people were only partially successful. A few feast days are no longer celebrated with the pomp they once were, but many Puerto Rican municipalities continue to hold public celebrations for a variety of Catholic holidays, while U.S. civic holidays have simply been added alongside these older celebrations.

The island's Catholicism played a large role in the independence movement since prominent Nationalist leaders, particularly Pedro Albizu Campos, tended to equate Catholicism with Puerto Rican culture and claimed that the United States was attempting to undermine the church and impose Protestantism on the population as a way to Americanize the island. For this reason, many on the Left were as fiercely Catholic, and in some cases more so, than conservatives. For example, many Nationalists and labor leaders objected to allowing women access to birth control in the century following the Treaty of Paris because it contradicted Catholic doctrine, while some pro-statehood leaders on the Right favored broadening access to birth control, including abortion after 1974, to fight the overpopulation that they believed was limiting economic development. Protestants have also had an impact on other aspects of Island politics, particularly the Episcopal Church, which has taken on a leadership role in the growing environmental movement.

In addition to Catholicism and a growing Protestant movement, another religion practiced on the island is Santería, a blending of the Catholic practice of revering saints with customs and beliefs from the religion of the Yoruba people, slaves who originally lived in the area of Africa that makes up modern-day Nigeria. The religion is called Santería because it involves the worship of saints who resemble Yuroba gods. Though the religion originally served as a way for African slaves to maintain their religion under the guise of adhering to the religion of their owners, today many Hispanics throughout Latin America and the United States say that they adhere to both religions—Santería and Christianity—simultaneously and see no contradiction in doing so. Santería has some regional variations. In Puerto Rico most adherents worship a central deity and a group of lesser gods called the Seven African Powers or *Siete Potencias*. The practice sometimes includes the sacrifice of animals, but adherents say that the animals, typically chickens, are killed humanely and eaten afterward.

Women's Suffrage

The women's suffrage movement on the island, active since the late 1800s, has often been depicted as primarily a movement of middle-class educated women, its leaders tending to argue that only educated, literate men and women should have the vote. In 1904 when universal male suffrage was instituted, for example, many elite and middle-class Puerto Rican suffragists argued that if uneducated men could vote then surely educated women should have the same right. However, working-class women were also fighting for the right to vote and it was a working-class woman who staged one of the most audacious challenges to the prohibition on women's suffrage. After women were given the right to vote in the United States, Genara Pagin, a Puerto Rican garment worker who had been living in the States returned to the island and attempted to vote in the island's 1920 elections. The U.S. Department of the Interior, which at that time was overseeing bureaucratic policy for the island, ruled that since Puerto Rico was not part of the United States, the latest amendment to the U.S. Constitution did not apply there. Educated women were given the vote in Puerto Rico in 1932 and all women were finally able to exercise that right in 1936.

It has been hypothesized that the vote was kept from women until the later 1930s because working women made up such a large part of the labor movement on the island and many in the business community feared that they were more radicalized than the men. Allowing them to take part in elections might skew the vote in favor of the socialists or the independence parties. According to some political historians, the decision of the conservative pro-statehood Republicans to form an alliance with the Socialist Party in the 1930s may have been motivated by the number of votes the Republicans thought they could gain from the Socialist and pro-labor vote once women were given the vote. The alliance created the pro-statehood Union, the forerunner of today's pro-statehood New Progressive Party.

Other historians have argued that *machismo* is so ingrained in Puerto Rican culture that U.S. intervention was necessary to bring about women's suffrage. Machismo is a cultural emphasis on masculinity and the public-directed role of the male head of household, and its counterpart, an emphasis on passive domestic-focused femininity, sometimes referred to *marianismo*, that is prevalent in many Latin American cultures. By this argument, of course, no Latin American countries would have female suffrage. Though there are countries that still deny the vote to women, none are found in Latin America.

ACTIVISM AND REPRESSION

Following the enactment of the Jones Act, many advised the President to appoint a Puerto Rican as governor. Instead he appointed Montgomery Reily, an inexperienced, low-level civil servant who proceeded to appoint friends and cronies with no knowledge of Puerto Rico to the island's most important posts. The Puerto Rican Senate refused to confirm many of them and even began impeachment proceedings to oust the governor, a power it did not seem to have, according to either Foraker or Jones. Reily was also being investigated by a U.S. grand jury for unrelated fiscal irregularities. Before he was replaced by Governor Horace Towner, Reily declared that expressing support for independence for Puerto Rico was a form of treason, because it advocated the overthrow of the U.S. government. He also announced that raising or bearing a Puerto Rican flag was a form of treasonous expression. These proclamations would be revisited during the anti-communist fervor that swept through the United States and found its way to Puerto Rico in the 1940s and 1950s, when a series of U.S. governors would use repressive tactics to silence dissent.

Throughout the 1920s, the legislature tried to reform the Jones Act to create more autonomy. Led by the newly named Alianza (Alliance) Party (formerly the Federalist and then Union Party), the legislature passed law after law designed to increase the elected government's autonomy and limit the power of the U.S. government in island affairs; however, all of them were vetoed by the governor, U.S. Congress, or the President. Finally, the Alianza Party disintegrated and became the Liberal Party, with Luis Muñoz Marín, Muñoz Rivera's son as one of its founding members. The conservative pro-statehood party banded together as the Coalición.

THE DEPRESSION AND THE NEW DEAL

The 1930s were a period of crisis in the relationship between the United States and Puerto Rico. Incomes dropped, conditions for many of the country's rural and urban poor became desperate, and a series of governors with military backgrounds chose to answer the discontent of the people with escalating law-and-order measures aimed at silencing the populace's calls for independence and economic justice.

The worldwide economic downturn hit Puerto Rico hard. As the fortunes of its only major trading partner, the United States, fell, Puerto Rico's economy crumbled. Income fell 30 percent between 1930 and 1933. By 1937 unemployment hit 60 percent. Isolated strikes broke out in several towns and industries. However, a popular governor kept the Puerto Rican discontent from erupting during the early years of the economic and humanitarian crisis. Though he failed to obtain the public funds he sought to alleviate poverty, Governor Theodore Roosevelt Jr., son of the twenty-sixth president, became the first governor to publicly discuss Puerto Rico's economic problems and to place the blame for them on failed U.S. policy, rather than on the innately poor character of the Puerto Rican people. Since he could not convince the federal government to send adequate aid during his short tenure of 1930 to 1932, Roosevelt tried to raise funds to alleviate hunger and supply medicines from the U.S. private sector. He also endeavored to learn Spanish. Though the charitable donations he amassed were inadequate and his Spanish famously awkward and full of errors, his honesty, his attempts to alleviate suffering, and his sincere collaboration with local leaders, along with his respectful attitude toward Puerto Rican culture endeared him to the Puerto Rican people. The fact that he was one of the island's most popular appointed governors demonstrates just how little effort most previous and subsequent U.S. governors exerted toward trying to understand the island they governed.

It was at this point that Muñoz Rivera's son Luis Muñoz Marín entered the political scene. Born months before the U.S. invasion of 1898 and educated in the United States, he returned to the island in 1931. At first he joined the Liberal Party and deferred to its senior members. However, he soon grew weary of the endless debates over status. None of the alternatives—statehood versus independence versus some form of reformed autonomous relationship with the United States—mattered, Muñoz Marín argued, as long as the United States was unwilling to grant them and as long as the vast majority of the population remained impoverished and uneducated. Muñoz Marín decided that the country needed to improve its infrastructure and economic base before it could address the status issue. According to Muñoz Marín, if Puerto Rico was given independence under the drastic conditions of the 1930s, it would not be able to sustain itself and its people would sink into even greater poverty. Discouraged by the leadership of the Liberal Party, which seemed to him obsessed with the status issue, Muñoz Marín returned to the States in the hopes that funds could be raised to ease suffering and create jobs.

The Depression continued to drive migration from Puerto Rico to the United States, even though it was well known that there were few jobs on the mainland and that people there were suffering as well. Food prices were a major driving force for migration to the United States in the 1930s as Puerto Rico continued to import the bulk of its food supply. Prices on most of the major staples that made up the working Puerto Rican's diet were 8 percent to 14 percent higher in Puerto Rico than they were in New York City. At the same time, wages in New York City were four to ten times higher. Many families felt they had no choice but to move to the new Puerto Rican *colonias* in New York, Chicago, and Boston. This migration would become even more intense during the industrial war effort of World War II.

The Puerto Rico Emergency Relief Administration (PRERA), part of President Franklin Roosevelt's New Deal policy designed to alleviate suffering and to address the underlying causes of the Depression by investing in infrastructure and stimulating new industries, was supposed to start operations in 1933. However, the conservative governors who had been helming Puerto Rico since the creation of the New Deal did everything in their power to block the distribution of aid to workers. Even before PRERA was created, Puerto Rico could have applied for funds through the Federal Emergency Relief Administration. However, Puerto Rico's anti-New Deal governor, Robert Gore, refused to apply, depriving the people of aid for which they were eligible.

In 1934, with the economy still faltering, a widespread general strike affected most of the sugar industry. The strikers rejected the agreement that the pro-union party negotiated for them and insisted that revolutionary leader Pedro Albizu Campos negotiate for them instead. Meanwhile, Puerto Ricans throughout the island showed support for the striking sugar workers by boycotting gasoline and electric power. The strike forced the U.S. administrators and their pro-statehood Puerto Rican legislative allies to rethink their policy of withholding aid. They began to distribute aid from PRERA. The more conservative elements in the U.S. federal government and Governor Blanton Winship favored installing harsh civic measures to go with the welfare provisions. Aid would come at the price of increased surveillance and curtailed expression. In part, Winship and his pro-business allies feared the enthusiasm Albizu Campos stirred whenever he spoke. Their aim was to curtail the independence and pro-worker movements. For the time being, President Roosevelt was willing to trust their strategy.

In 1934, Muñoz Marín, still residing in the United States, used his connections to meet with economists Carlos Chardon and Rexford Guy Tugwell, and the President's wife, Eleanor Roosevelt, all of whom were concerned that the people of Puerto Rico were not getting the relief they needed. In response to their concerns, President Roosevelt authorized a Puerto Rican Policy Commission to study the island's needs. The strategy the commission created has been called the Chardon Plan. It proposed reorienting the Puerto Rican economy away from large industrial farms toward smaller family farms, diversifying the economy, weaning Puerto Rican endeavors from U.S. investment and ownership, and creating industrial sectors based on local resources. Roosevelt placed Chardon in charge of dispersing funds from PRERA and other New Deal initiatives on the island, despite Governor Winship's objections. Through Chardon's efficiency, 35 percent of Puerto Ricans received some form of PRERA aid by the middle of 1934. With some reluctance, Winship tolerated Chardon's implementation of Roosevelt's program on the island and concentrated his activities on maintaining law and order along with his police commissioner, Francis E. Riggs, whose brutal tactics made him and the governor unpopular with many segments of the population.

THE INDEPENDENCE MOVEMENT AND THE PONCE MASSACRE

In 1926 the Nationalist Party sent Pedro Albizu Campos, a Harvard-educated lawyer, on a four-year journey through the Caribbean and Latin America, where he became increasingly radicalized, dedicated to a mission of independence for Puerto Rico and anti-colonial struggle for all oppressed peoples. Albizu, who was of Afro-Puerto Rican ancestry had also served as an officer in an African American unit of the U.S. Army during World War I.

When he returned from his four-year journey across Latin America on May 12, 1930, the Nationalists elected Albizu Campos party president. More radicalized than ever by his time meeting with revolutionaries throughout the Spanish-speaking world, Albizu stated that the independence movement would be justified in the use of violence to achieve their goals if necessary. Further, he argued, it was the responsibility of the people to actively work toward independence, and not simply wait passively for the United States to grant Puerto Rico its sovereignty. After the Nationalist Party's disappointing showing in the 1932 elections, Albizu advocated a strategy of unrest that would entice the United States to relinquish its association with the troublesome island. In addition to Albizu's involvement with the sugar strike of 1934, the independence leader drew large crowds wherever he spoke and ignored Winship's injunctions against raising the Puerto Rican flag. In defiance of the governor's injunctions against free speech, Albizu delivered passionate arguments for Puerto Rican independence wherever and whenever he appeared.

On October 24, 1935, Albizu was scheduled to speak at the University of Puerto Rico's Río Piedras campus. Authorities decided a large police presence was necessary to prevent any unrest. A car carrying Nationalist Party members was stopped and the occupants arrested, allegedly for carrying bombs. On the way to the police station, four of the Nationalists and one bystander were killed. Albizu and his party vowed revenge for the murdered Nationalists. On February 23, 1936, Police Commissioner Riggs was assassinated. Two young Nationalists were accused of his murder and arrested. Both were killed in jail during an alleged attempt to escape. Albizu and seven other Nationalist Party leaders were charged with sedition and plotting to overthrow the U.S. government. Albizu Campos and his fellow party members were sent to prison in Atlanta, Georgia, for 15 years.

While Alibizu was in prison, in 1937 the Nationalists asked the mayor of Ponce for permission to hold a march on March 12, which he granted. The chief of police revoked the mayor's permit. Party leaders decided to march anyway. Police fired on the crowd that had gathered for the march. In all, 19 people were killed, including two police officers, and more than 100 people were wounded. In the aftermath of what became known as the Ponce Massacre, more than 10,000 showed up at the funeral for the demonstrators and 3,000 gathered in East Harlem to hear Albizu Campos's lawyer explain what little he knew about the matter. Repercussions were wide-ranging. Not only were Nationalist Party members monitored and punished, but Liberal Party members faced retaliation from the U.S. governor as well. For example, Chardon was removed from his position as head of PRERA. In response to Winship's crackdown, a 37-day dockworkers' strike was held that paralyzed shipping and commerce across the island. Despite the tense political climate, Governor Winship decided to hold a parade on July 25, 1938, to commemorate the 1898 U.S. invasion. The celebration was interrupted by gunfire and dozens were wounded, including government officials. A detective was killed when he leaped in front of a bullet intended for Winship. At this point, President Roosevelt began to realize that Winship's leadership was actually contributing to unrest, rather than containing it. He offered the post of governor to Navy Admiral William Leahy.

The era of the collaboration between law-and-order governors and conservative pro-statehood party members was coming to an end and Puerto Ricans would soon enjoy a more active role in their own governance. This new autonomy would fall short of either statehood or independence. The architect of this middle path would be Luis Muñoz Marín.

THE RISE OF THE POPULAR DEMOCRATIC PARTY

During Muñoz Marín's years in the United States, he studied the workings of government and economics, knowledge he would use to reach his political goals of alleviating Puerto Rico's poverty and increasing its political autonomy. His shift toward political and economic autonomy over independence as a realistic political goal was largely shaped by events following the assassination of Police Commissioner Riggs.

In 1936, U.S. Senator Millard Tydings drafted a bill that called for a Puerto Rican plebiscite (referendum) that would allow islanders to vote for or against independence. The catch was that if the majority of Puerto Ricans voted for independence they could not receive any aid from the United States and would be burdened with large trade tariffs. This bill was designed as a punishment for Puerto Rico's ingratitude and lawlessness. Given Puerto Rico's dependency on U.S. investment and trade, the bill would have crushed the Puerto Rican people. Though the bill never moved out of committee, Muñoz Marín noted the enthusiasm with which many U.S. political leaders drafted and praised the proposal. He was convinced that the United States would not allow for a gentle transition toward independence for his country and that the island's economy was not developed enough to stand on its own.

It was in this context that Muñoz Marín returned to Puerto Rico. Meeting with members of his Liberal Party he stated that Puerto Rico was not ready for independence, words that rankled his fellow party members, who expelled him from their ranks. In response to his expulsion, on July 22, 1937, Muñoz Marín formed the Popular Democratic Party (PDP). He chose as the party's emblem the *jibaro*, or mountain peasant, whose most literal translation in English may be something like "hillbilly." At rallies and marches, members of the party chose to wear the straw hats that *jibaros* wore while working in the sun. The party's motto, "Bread, Land, and Freedom," communicated the order of its priorities—first food, clothing, education, and other necessities, then land and capital redistribution to strengthen Puerto Ricans' stake in their country's economy, and only then independence, or at the very least, a form of autonomist government that would restore Puerto Rican dignity. It was a message that played well among the country's most impoverished voters, whose need to feed and shelter their families outweighed less immediate and abstract arguments over political status.

The PDP emerged at a time when many members of the legislature and other local governing bodies were controlled by wealthy sugar plantation owners whose interests were closely aligned with U.S. business. The voters, especially in the agricultural regions, were so uneducated, desperately poor, and new to the democratic process that they often sold their votes for $5 or a pair of shoes to the ever-evolving pro-U.S. party (the Republicans, the Alianza, etc.; the names changed frequently while the key actors and policies remained fairly constant). To combat vote selling, Muñoz Marín implemented what he had learned from observing activists and political parties in the United States, creating a grassroots political movement for increased local rule throughout the rural areas. Muñoz Marín convinced the sugar cane workers and other agricultural wage earners to refuse bribes and express their patriotism by casting their vote and placing a majority of Popular Democratic party members in the legislature during the 1940 elections. Muñoz Marín and the PDP would retain their majority in the legislature for the next 28 years.

WORLD WAR II

Following Governor Winship's ouster, Governor William Leahy concentrated on preparing the island for its possible role in World War II, overseeing the quick construction of several military bases and leaving most matters of internal governance up to local officials.

After the Japanese bombed Hawaii's Pearl Harbor, large numbers of young Puerto Rican men living on the island and in the U.S. *colonias* of New York, Chicago, Boston, and elsewhere volunteered to fight in the U.S. Army. Puerto Ricans in the United States were assigned to either African American or white units depending on their perceived race. Many of the Puerto Ricans living on the island who volunteered for service fought in the 65th Infantry Regiment. Called the "Borinquineers," this highly decorated unit fought in Europe. Other Puerto Ricans, along with large numbers of other Spanish-speakers of other nationalities, were sent to the Philippines, where it was believed their language skills might be useful. Many Puerto Rican recruits on the island and in the States were taken aback when Army officials asked them to line up and take off their shirts so that they could be segregated into African American and white units by the color of the skin on their backs.

Leahy, who was named U.S. Ambassador to France was replaced as governor by Rexford Tugwell. Following the widespread strikes of the 1930s and the austere actions Governor Winship had taken to suppress pro-independence rhetoric, tensions between U.S. administrators and the Puerto Ricans they governed were running high. This increasing tension was about to shift under the leadership of Governor Tugwell, who served as Puerto Rico's last U.S.-born governor from 1942 to 1946. Tugwell, an economist, had been studying the island for years and had already formed a working relationship with some of the island's leading young reformers, particularly Muñoz Marín. He was also an enthusiastic New Dealer who had favored Chardon's plan to diversify the local economy. For the next several years, Tugwell and Muñoz Marín formed a partnership, splitting various governmental functions between them and quickly implementing sweeping changes in economics, education, politics, agriculture, health care, and nearly every other aspect of life on the island.

Fortifications built by the Spanish in the sixteenth century can be clearly seen in this modern aerial view of the Old San Juan section of the island's capital. [Photo provided by the Puerto Rico Tourism Company]

Indigenous Taíno artists created thousands of "three-pointers," elaborately carved triangular objects believed to have religious significance. [Della Zuana Pascal/Corbis Sygma]

This seventeenth-century engraving depicts Puerto Rico as visualized by a Spanish illustrator. [Courtesy of the Library of Congress]

Ponce de Leon.

Kapitel VIII.

Florida.

Juan Ponce de Leon, the first governor of Puerto Rico, is believed to have come to the New World during Christopher Columbus' Second Voyage in 1493. [Courtesy of the Library of Congress]

During the Golden Age of Piracy, pirates used grappling hooks to attack ships in the Spanish flotilla. [Bettmann/Corbis]

THE SPANISH-AMERICAN TREATY OF PEACE, PARIS DEC. 10TH 1898.

In the aftermath of the Spanish-American War and U.S. invasion of Puerto Rico, Spain ceded Puerto Rico to the United States as part of the Treaty of Paris in 1898. [Courtesy of the Library of Congress]

Nationalist leader Pedro Albizu Campos is arrested after the 1950 Uprising, a series of gun battles between pro-independence activists and law enforcement officials that included the attempted assassinations of U.S. President Harry Truman and Puerto Rico Governor Luis Muñoz Marín. [AP Photo]

Demonstrators march outside the U.S. Navy bombing range in Vieques in May 2000. In 1999, a military accident killed a civilian guard, spurring years of protests calling for the United States to end weapons testing and close its military base on the island. The base was closed in 2004. [AP Photo/Ricardo Figueroa]

Governor Sila M. Calderon became the first woman elected to Puerto Rico's highest office in 2001. [AP Photo/Ricky Arduengo]

On June 24, 2009, Puerto Rico Governor Luis Guillermo Fortuño-Burset testified before the U.S. House Committee on Natural Resources on behalf of the Puerto Rico Democracy Act, a bill that would create an island-wide referendum on Puerto Rico's status, the fourth since 1967. [AP Photo/Harry Hamburg]

6

Commonwealth: The Freely Associated State of Puerto Rico (1948–1968)

THE LEAD UP TO COMMONWEALTH STATUS

Governor Rexford Tugwell and Luis Muñoz Marín, president of the Puerto Rican Senate, were aided in their endeavors to transform the island's economy from one dominated by a few large landowners to more diversified industrial base by a wartime shortage of distilled liquor. Puerto Rico's ability to produce rum for the United States and its allies ended up paying for many of the island's wartime reforms. Between 1941 and 1946, Puerto Rico received about $160,000 million in extra revenue thanks to the worldwide liquor shortage. Aided by the rum funds, the Puerto Rican government, following through on the provisions of Chardon's original plans before he was removed as head of the Puerto Rico Emergency Relief Administration (PRERA), took over hundreds of acres of land that violated a previously ignored law that prohibited foreign entities from owning more than 500 acres of land, compensating owners for the value of their lost land. Some of the land was divided into small plots and given to farm workers rent-free. The farmers, who did not hold the mortgages on the land, were encouraged to grow food for their families and communities in the hope that the policy might slowly ease some of the island's dependence on U.S. food imports and create a more diversified agricultural base. Tugwell and Muñoz Marín feared that if they gave the deeds for the land to workers they would simply sell them back to large wealthy landowners or foreign interests. By the end of the 1950s, more than 50,000 families had been resettled onto these small government-owned lots. Though these farmers did not have enough land to become wealthy or even free from the need to supplement their income with wage work, they were freed from rent and the threat of eviction.

Most of the confiscated land was maintained as government-owned large-scale sugar, coffee, or tobacco plantations and processing centers, which were run as cooperatives for workers who provided the labor and shared in the profits. Most sugar plantations were still owned by elite families and the sugar industry continued to grow until a gradual decline began during the 1950s. The land reform program did not substantially change the nature of land ownership on the island and it did not succeed in creating a diversified agricultural sector or in weaning Puerto Rico from its dependence on U.S. food imports.

Another element of the economic plan was the creation of industries. At first, Muñoz Marín hoped to use locally available raw materials to forge an industrial base and export economy. The factories would be financed and owned by the government with workers sharing in profits. The first endeavors included a glass and bottle factory, paper and box plant, ceramics and clay products producer, and a shoe manufacturer. Eventually, Muñoz Marín abandoned the project in favor of a new, more ambitious endeavor, Operation Bootstrap, aimed at attracting foreign investment and transforming Puerto Rico into an industrial center.

PUERTO RICO'S FIRST PUERTO RICAN GOVERNORS

Tugwell and Muñoz Marín's industrial projects were attacked by the island's pro-capitalist segments, including plantation and distillery owners, merchants, and pro-statehood newspapers and politicians, who boycotted the products created in the government-owned plants. However, the policies were popular with the workers and in November 1944, Muñoz Marín's Popular Democratic Party (PDP) won 65 percent of the vote. In 1946, President Harry Truman appointed PDP member Jesús T. Piñero the first Puerto Rican-born governor of the island. In 1947, the legislature enacted a law calling for the governor to be elected, which was approved by Congress, and in 1948 Muñoz Marín won over 60 percent of the vote to become the first democratically elected governor of Puerto Rico. He was sworn in on January 2, 1949.

COMMONWEALTH STATUS

In 1947, nationalist Pedro Albizu Campos returned to Puerto Rico. On the day of his arrival, students at the University of Puerto Rico raised the Puerto Rican flag and were subsequently expelled, since under Governor Winship this action had been ruled as illegal political speech advocating the overthrow of the U.S. government. A student strike followed. In the aftermath of the conflict the Puerto Rican legislature adopted a law, sometimes called the Gag Law, reiterating former Governor Winship's order that prohibited speech advocating the violent overthrow of the U.S. government. The Gag Law, which was signed into law by Governor Piñero in 1948, criminalized any discussion of possible independence for Puerto Rico and displaying the Puerto Rican flag.

That year, Puerto Rico sent its own team to the Olympic Games, marching under a flag bearing the Olympic rings since it would have been illegal at that time for them to march under the Puerto Rican flag. All subsequent Puerto Rican Olympic teams have marched bearing the Puerto Rican flag.

Muñoz Marín knew that the U.S. government was fearful of the possibility that either the Socialist wing of the pro-statehood party or the independence movement might gain popularity among the Puerto Rican people. Banking on this fear and his own popularity he hoped the timing might be favorable to renegotiate the nature of governing conditions between the United States and the island. The form of government Muñoz Marín negotiated with Congress is officially called the *Estado Libre Asociado* (Freely Associated State).

Muñoz Marín wrote Public Law 600, setting up the structure that allowed for the drafting of the constitution and the establishment of the Commonwealth, or Freely Associated State. Public Law 600 was vehemently criticized by the pro-independence Nationalist Party for stating that the U.S. Congress would approve the constitution, thus negating the law's stated claim that the new status would be adopted "in the nature of a compact" and under the principle of a "government by consent." Nevertheless, the referendum initiating the drafting of the constitution was approved by a majority of voters on the island on June 4, 1951. The constitution, which was drafted by elected representatives under Muñoz Marín's guidance from September 1951 to February 1952, changed the form of the insular government and included an extensive Bill of Rights.

Once the constitution was drafted, it needed to be approved by Congress, a process many expected to be a formality since the constitution had adhered closely to the guidelines for constitutional government set up by the United Nations. However, during the hearings that led to the constitution's ratification, Muñoz Marín was repeatedly forced to assure members of Congress threatening to withhold their approval of the constitution and commonwealth status that the United States could amend or change the relationship at any time and that upholding the constitution would not change the body's power to unilaterally alter the U.S.–Puerto Rico relationship at any time. In addition, Congressional members expressed their concern about statements Muñoz Marín had made in the past, many of which implied that, without a constitution representing consent by the people to live in association with the people of the United States, Puerto Rico would essentially remain a colony. Various members of Congress argued that Puerto Rico had never been a colony of the United States because it had never been called a colony and further that it could not have been a colony because the United States has never had and would not have colonies. As the rhetoric of the Congressional committee meetings deteriorated, Muñoz Marín's former colleague Rexford Tugwell urged him to acquiesce to any rhetorical concessions the Congressional leaders might insist on to get the constitution ratified. In this context, Muñoz Marín agreed with the U.S. leaders that Puerto Rico had not in fact ever been a U.S. colony, a concession that nearly cost him his life.

The Puerto Rican constitutional convention reconvened to make the required changes and the constitution and the new Commonwealth status allowing for internal self-rule was proclaimed July 25, 1952, nearly 54 years after U.S. troops had landed on Puerto Rico.

NATIONALIST INSURRECTION

Most Puerto Ricans were encouraged by the creation of the *Estado Libre Asociado*. Eighty percent voted to ratify it in a 1952 referendum, and its declaration, along with the ratification of the Constitution, was celebrated with marches and patriotic festivals throughout the island.

The process also satisfied the U.N. General Assembly, which after some debate decided that the new constitution and Commonwealth status represented a new government relationship that reflected the will of the people and, therefore, relieved the United States from its duty of reporting annually on Puerto Rico's progress toward self-government.

However, during the two-year process that led to the declaration of the new status, many argued that calling the new governance system a Freely Associated State was misleading and legally inaccurate, since an act of Congress had been needed to allow Puerto Rico to draft the constitution that was meant to declare the island's free status. After the constitution was drafted by the Puerto Rican congress, the U.S. Congress demanded changes, including the addition of a provision stating that the United States could change the nature of the relationship at any time in any manner it saw fit without the input of the Puerto Rican government or voters. Further, under its new status Puerto Rico was still not a state or an incorporated territory. As many pro-state and pro-independence advocates pointed out, Puerto Rico's constitution placed it no closer to independence or statehood than it had been before. The Nationalists were especially angered by the process and by Muñoz Marín's concessions that Puerto Rico was not and had never been a U.S. colony.

In the midst of the hearings and referendums surrounding the creation of the Commonwealth, on October 30 and November 1, 1950, independence forces unhappy with the process engaged in a series of violent uprisings in various sections of the island that included an attempted assassination of Governor Muñoz Marín at La Fortaleza; an attempted assassination of U.S. President Harry Truman in Blair House in New York City (where he was staying while the White House was undergoing repairs); and attacks by bands of protestors in seven towns on the island, capturing one of them, Jayuya, and declaring the existence of the republic in a move reminiscent of El Grito de Lares, while in another town rebels burned down the police station and the post office.

In all, 28 people, including nine Nationalists, were killed and 49 people wounded in what came to be called the Nationalist Insurrection of 1950. The coordinated attacks were supposed to take place later and after more planning, but this strategy was thwarted when police confiscated weapons from Albizu Campos' car on October 27, 1950. After Albizu Campos was arrested, his deputies had to act without his guidance and before all the preparations were complete. Otherwise attacks might have been more widespread and even more deadly. After order was restored in the weeks that followed, as many as 140 Nationalists were arrested and Albizu Campos was jailed again. He was released in 1953. But in 1954, Nationalists in Washington, D.C., sprayed bullets into the House of Representatives from the spectator gallery, wounding five Congressmen. In the aftermath of the Congressional shooting, Albizu Campos was arrested again and jailed until 1964. He died in 1965.

OPERATION BOOTSTRAP

Even prior to his election as governor, Muñoz Marín had launched a new aggressive platform of his economic plan, called Operation Bootstrap (*Operación Manos a la Obra*) in 1947, in his capacity as president of the legislature. Tagged "the battle for production," the policy's aim was to attract foreign investment in industrialized endeavors at a rate fast enough to make up for the island's shrinking agricultural sector. It was hoped that the new enterprises would quickly enhance employment and provide higher paying jobs. Taking advantage of tax loopholes that already existed thanks to Puerto Rico's unprecedented status, adding on other local tax breaks, and building facilities that corporations could lease rent-free, Muñoz Marín hoped to entice industries to relocate to Puerto Rico. In addition, by placing their manufacturing facilities on what was technically U.S. soil, the industries were given free access to U.S. markets.

Puerto Ricans would thus be christened into the new global industrial economy and gain marketable skills. They would be paid at rates that might seem cheap to the incoming industries but would be significantly higher than the earnings of sugar or tobacco workers. The high income levels would improve the quality of life for thousands of Puerto Ricans.

To accomplish these goals, Muñoz Marín set up the Economic Development Administration (its Spanish acronym was FOMENTO) to attract foreign and U.S. industrial investment. After an initially slow start, the policy took off, catching the first wave of the post-war economic expansion and allowing Muñoz Marín to fill most of the buildings his government had built in the hopes of attracting tenants. By 1950 over 90 plants were located on the island; by the mid-1960s there were over 900. In 1956, manufacturing income exceeded agricultural income for the first time in the island's history. The workers employed by these overseas entities enjoyed rapid improvements in their standard of living.

There were downsides: once foreign companies set up shop many refused to pay the agreed-on prices for facilities that had not been built to their specifications. Though the rent and lease prices were lower than any comparable facilities in the world at that time, corporations haggled and were given concessions. In addition, the bulk of industries were not locally owned or locally managed. The textile, food products, and consumer goods industries that dominated the program shipped in raw materials, which were assembled on the island and then shipped out. The Puerto Ricans were serving as a ready, inexpensive source of labor for outsiders, many of whom did not live on the island, and therefore did not pay significant taxes on the island or even engage in civic projects. Some critics contend that Operation Bootstrap only succeeded in attracting labor-intensive, low technology industries that paid low wages and held no loyalty toward their workers. When trade barriers to the U.S. market eased in the 1970s and 1980s, the industries left to seek even cheaper sources of labor and more generous tax breaks elsewhere. Despite the enormous efforts that went into Operation Bootstrap and the island's other industrial initiatives, job creation barely kept pace with the rate of job loss from a diminishing agricultural sector. Losses probably would have exceeded gains and led to high levels of chronic unemployment if not for the massive numbers of Puerto Ricans who were migrating to the States.

Although it is true that no integrated markets based on local raw materials emerged, the policy transformed the island from an agricultural monoculture—that is, an economy that produced one major crop, sugar, and had very little diversity or sustainability—to an export-focused manufacturing economy. By the 1950s, an increasing number of Puerto Ricans became urban dwellers and fewer lived in the rural areas. The geographic concentration of jobs in a few key urban centers led to suburban development as workers commuted between their homes and work. Traffic, pollution, and reliance on oil became issues of concern. Despite these problems, for many Puerto Ricans, living standards improved throughout the 1950s and 1960s. Wages increased as did life expectancy. New roads, electrical grids, and housing were built. The education and health care systems expanded and became more accessible for a larger percentage of the population and the literacy rate approached 90 percent.

MIGRATION

During World War II, the United States encouraged and even paid for many Puerto Ricans to come to the States to work in the munitions industry and other sectors of the industrial war effort. After the war, the pace of migration continued to increase, especially in the 1950s as air travel made migration increasingly easy and affordable. It has been estimated that migration from the island to the States from 1950 to 1970 was between 25 percent and 30 percent of the population.

Over the years the government has cited overpopulation as the reason for its persistent unemployment problem and encouraged migration as one way to address it. In the post-war era, the government created the Department of Labor, which negotiated agreements with stateside agricultural and industrial employers in states like Connecticut, Massachusetts, and New Jersey.

The rising popularity and affordability of air travel also made it easier for Puerto Ricans to visit family members or move back to the island in what has come to be called a circular migration pattern. Air travel also contributed to Puerto Rico's rise as a tourist destination, especially after the 1959 Cuban Revolution. Another factor that helped increase tourism to Puerto Rico and the rest of the Caribbean after World War II was the rise of a large middle class in the United States, Canada, and Europe with the means to travel overseas for pleasure.

FAMILY PLANNING

Another solution to the overpopulation problem was family planning. This took several forms, all of which angered the dominant Catholic

Church. Some feminist-based nonprofit sources focused on birth control and sexual/reproductive agency for women. However, there is a darker component to the island's family planning history. With the government's permission, pharmaceutical companies used Puerto Rico as a testing ground for new forms of birth control. Many women have since said that they did not know that the medication they were taking was being tested and had not yet been approved for the U.S. market. Other organizations encouraged sterilization, including hospitals, which would perform tubal ligations (a surgical procedure that cuts, burns, or otherwise blocks a woman's fallopian tubes so that eggs cannot be fertilized) during deliveries. At least one hospital would not perform deliveries of a mother's fourth child unless she agreed to sterilization at the same time. Many women who underwent sterilization during this period have since said that they were told that the procedures they underwent were temporary. Others have said the sterilizations were forced or coerced, that they were told that health care would be withheld from them and from their children if they did not agree to sterilizations. Some activists have claimed that sterilizations were disproportionally aimed at low-income and dark-skinned women, though the results of document analysis from family planning centers and hospitals have been inconclusive. What can be quantified is that by 1982, 39 percent of Puerto Rican women aged 15 to 49 were sterilized, the highest rate of any nation in the world.

THE FIRST PLEBISCITE, 1967

Held in 1967, the First Plebiscite, or referendum on the island's status, affirmed the PDP's Commonwealth government as the status preferred by Puerto Ricans living on the island, with 60 percent voting for Commonwealth. Despite the fact that officials from the pro-independence and pro-statehood factions had called for their supporters to boycott the vote, the strong showing in favor of Commonwealth status was evidence of the popularity of the PDP during what would prove to be the party's high mark. Living standards for most Puerto Ricans were still improving and most expected this trend to continue. Most voters were satisfied with their ability to vote for their own governor and legislature. Fewer everyday Puerto Ricans were concerned with their inability to vote in U.S. presidential elections than they might have been if the economic picture were more troubling, as it soon would be.

Cultural changes were evident, from the opening of the first supermarkets and malls, to the emergence of highways and suburbs, and most of them were welcomed. In addition to mass culture and pop culture, high culture was also experiencing a renaissance as artists were then fleeing both Francisco Franco's fascist regime and Castro's Cuba to settle in Puerto Rico. Musicians, artists, and writers from a variety of Lain American and Hispanic backgrounds mingled over cocktail parties in San Juan's new hirises, launched literary magazines, and raised Puerto Rico's cultural status in the Spanish-speaking world.

In 1964 Muñoz Marín declined to run for governor. His successor was fellow PDP leader Roberto Sánchez Vilella. During Vilella's four-year term divisions within the PDP grew over the direction of Operation Bootstrap and other issues. At the end of his term, Sanchez opted to run against the PDP's chosen candidate as a member of the Popular Vanguard, a splinter group that had parted ways with the PDP. Neither the PDP nor the Vanguard candidate won. Instead, Luis A. Ferré, an industrialist representing the latest statehood party, the New Progressives, won the governor's race. The PDP still controlled the majority of seats in the Senate, but Ferré's victory marked the first major electoral defeat for the PDP in three decades.

7

State of Transition: After Operation Bootstrap (1968–1998)

THE RISE OF THE NEW PROGRESSIVE PARTY

During the 1950s and 1960s, Operation Bootstrap brought large amounts of U.S. and foreign investment to the island, but wages did not increase at the same pace and manufacturing salaries on the island remained four or five times lower than those in the States. By the late 1960s the economy was not growing at the rate of the previous two decades and unemployment began to climb. By some estimates, foreign interests controlled up to 70 percent of the island's wealth.

Many Puerto Ricans blamed their problems on the moderate policies of a moderate leader, Muñoz Marín, whose ideas, many said, were outdated and not aggressive enough to keep pace with a faster-paced financial world. The worldwide recession of the 1970s underscored the island's dependency on the fortunes of the United States. Without a diversified economy and an equally diverse set of trading partners, economically Puerto Rico was as dependent on a single political entity as any colony. Still beloved for the dignity he had brought to the country at a critical time in its history, many believed the time of Muñoz Marín middle path of autonomy was past.

The dream of independence, still dear to many Puerto Ricans, seemed too risky. Statehood seemed within reach.

Leaders of the pro-statehood New Progressive Party (*Partido Nuevo Progresista* or PNP) suspected that growing fears about the economy and job market might lead some workers to reconsider their unconditional support for the Popular Democratic Party (PDP) in favor of a pro-statehood agenda. They were right. In 1968, Luis A. Ferré of the New Progressive Party defeated the PDP's candidate in the governor's race, the first defeat for the PDP since 1940.

For a while the electorate was torn and close elections went back and forth between the statehood party and the autonomists, often with one party in control of the executive and the other controlling the legislature. Governance required cooperation between the two main parties and the smaller independence movement utilized civil disobedience to communicate its concerns. Other interest groups were also making their concerns visible, including labor organizations, environmentalists, and feminists.

Realizing that the era's uncertain economic and social climate made the PDP vulnerable, pro-statehood leader Carlos Romero Barceló took the reins of the New Progressive Party, changing the tone of its political message to voters. He argued that the U.S. Civil Rights movement and the social safety net created by President Lyndon Johnson's Great Society would protect Puerto Ricans from losing their cultural identity and improve conditions for the poorest Puerto Ricans if the island became the fifty-first state. At the same time, the leadership of the New Progressive Party remained well-off and the platform pro-business. Romero Barceló was attempting to put together a coalition of varied interests that could trump the PDP's appeal to the working class and moderate liberal elites. It worked. The PNP controlled the governor's office as often as the PDP has in the decades that followed and frequently holds a majority or plurality of seats in the legislature as well. The two parties share nearly equal support from island voters, with a small percentage of voters, typically fewer than 10 percent, voting for pro-independence candidates. Romero Barceló served two terms as governor, from 1977 to 1985.

Some have seen the increased popularity of the pro-statehood theme in island politics from the late 1960s to the present as a testament to PDP's success and its failures. It can be argued that a more conservative, pro-business, pro-establishment group of young voters was made possible by the success of Operation Bootstrap, which allowed a growing number of young, educated Puerto Ricans to join the professional ranks as lawyers, doctors, teachers, scientists, and business managers. These young voters considered themselves middle-class capitalists and tended to see the PDP's New Deal ideals as outdated. They aspired to a North American lifestyle and income level, and believed that becoming part of the United States, on equal footing with other states, would achieve this.

MUÑOZ MARÍN'S FAILED PETROCHEMICAL STRATEGY

In addition to the worldwide economic downturn of the 1970s, the PDP's loss of power and popularity has been blamed on Muñoz Marín's failed plan to transform the island into a center for petrochemical enterprises, including oil refineries. Many in the U.S. Congress approved the strategy and had cleared the way for large amounts of raw oil to be imported to Puerto Rico. The most ambitious feature of the plan was the construction of an enormous deep water oil factory off the coast. But the project was stalled and ultimately derailed by new segments of society emerging in the 1970s, among them environmental activists. Had the scheme succeeded, the new revenue stream would have come at the cost of potential damage to the environment as well as to the tourism industry. The plan was also thwarted by a sharp increase in the cost of crude oil due to the oil crisis of the last 1970s. The sharp profits Muñoz Marín envisioned became less and less likely and nothing short of them would pay for the initial capital outlay the scheme required.

After Muñoz Marín's attempts to foster a petrochemical industry on the island failed, he scrambled to work with U.S. lawmakers to create tax incentives to attract pharmaceutical and electronics firms to the island, a venture that was successful on a limited scale, but did not bring in the number of jobs that the labor-intensive petrochemical strategy might have attracted.

Once the petrochemical scheme failed to materialize and unemployment continued to climb, voters aimed their frustrations at the PDP. Since the early 1970s, the United States has had several economic ups and downs, but Puerto Rico's economy has not recovered. Once globalization took hold in the 1970s, international corporations began moving manufacturing to cheaper regions of the world, particularly to countries where no protections were in place for workers. In these environments, corporations do not have to contend with minimum wages, occupational safety and environmental regulations, or legislation prohibiting the employment of children. Flexible trade agreements, such as the North American Free Trade Agreement, mean that industries that engage in these practices face no obstacles to markets. In this environment, Puerto Rico's relatively cheap labor cannot compete with countries where no legal controls exist to protect workers' basic human rights.

The gap in employment has been filled by light industry in the pharmaceutical and electronic consumer goods markets; an increase in white-collar jobs in the financial sector, government jobs, and tourism; and a large informal economy, which includes self-employment, off-the-books labor, and crime.

EFFECTS OF THE CUBAN REVOLUTION

The 1959 Cuban Revolution resulted in the ouster of leader Fulgencio Batista by Marxist forces led by Fidel Castro, his brother Raúl, and Argentine revolutionary Ernesto "Che" Guevara. This event had many consequences for Puerto Rico.

Following the revolution, many Cuban exiles settled in Puerto Rico, bringing with them new influences on art, language, food, music, and politics. More than fifty years after the revolution, the economic devastation caused by the U.S. trade embargo of Cuba continues to supply a steady stream of Cuban immigrants to Puerto Rico. The embargo also serves as a reminder of the vulnerability of small countries like Cuba in the face of the economic power of the United States. It is not unusual for Puerto Ricans to point to Cuba's weak economy as an example of what might happen if Puerto Rico does not retain its current political association with the United States.

Perhaps one of the most important consequences of the Cuban Revolution for Puerto Rico may have been the boost it gave tourism. Prior to the revolution, Cuba was a leading destination for U.S. tourists. Its luxury hotels and opulent casinos presented a stark contrast to the poverty that pervaded most of the island. With completion of the Luis Muñoz Marín International Airport in 1955, the construction of several luxury hotels along the coastline, and the legalization of gambling all established just prior to the 1959 revolution, Puerto Rico was poised to become the new playground for wealthy and middle-class U.S. travelers. The strategy worked. Today, tourism is one of Puerto Rico's leading industries, making up a little less than 6 percent of the gross domestic product and providing 73,000, or about one out of every 18, jobs on the island.[1]

In the 1960s and 1970s, younger members of the independence and labor movements adopted the Marxist ideology of Castro and Guevara, veering away from the pro-Catholic, pro-family rhetoric that had traditionally characterized those movements. This Marxist influence seemed to subside after the 1970s as new social movements—feminism and environmentalism— became more prominent.

GREEN, FEMINIST, AND GAY ACTIVISTS

Beginning in the 1960s many Puerto Ricans began to question the ecological costs of industrialization. In 1967, for example, the Episcopal Church sponsored the formation of the influential Misión Industrial. Groups representing the interests of labor increasingly adopted environmentalism as part of their agenda, calling for an end to the exploitation of Puerto Rican resources by foreign corporations. By the late 1960s criticism from a broad range of organizations forced the government to abandon plans to allow foreign corporations to mine for copper in the interior sections of the island. Similar protests were partly responsible for the government's decision to halt the most ambitious aspects of its plans to foster petrochemical industries in the 1970s. Today, environmental activists continue to monitor development by industry and the tourist sector, demanding that government prioritize safeguards for the island's natural resources when making decisions. One of the movement's most pressing concerns is the prediction by some scientists that global warming will raise sea levels and increase the frequency and strength of hurricanes throughout the Caribbean.

During the 1960s and 1970s, cross-migration between U.S. and island-born Puerto Ricans had a hand in island protest movements, particularly in a radicalizing trend among the youth, who no longer looked to an older generation for leadership, but began movements and organizations of their own to express their concerns. Inspired by the anti-war movement on college campuses in the United States, many Puerto Rican students began protesting the Vietnam War and questioning the legitimacy of the draft in light of Puerto Rico's political status and the inability of Puerto Ricans to vote for the President, who determines war policy, or for a voting delegation to the U.S. Congress that funds military engagements and institutes military drafts. By the early 1970s, many young Puerto Ricans on the island were especially inspired by the Young Lords, a political organization started by Puerto Ricans living in New York. Though the group initially patterned themselves after the Black Panthers, their agenda quickly evolved to embrace a wider range of social justice concerns, particularly issues of gender equity.

The long-dormant feminist movement re-emerged on the island in the 1970s. Prior to that, feminists had been active during the suffrage movement of the 1920s and 1930s. After all women were granted the vote in 1936, pockets of feminist activists remained, many of them working to ensure women access to birth control, while other former suffragettes took government and nonprofit posts that allowed them to work with impoverished women and children, increasing access to education and health care. However, the movement remained small and relatively silent until the 1970s, when it was rekindled by the U.S. women's movement and dissatisfaction among women in the labor movement over wage inequality and other issues of equity in the workplace.

Another issue that spurred feminists to speak out was the nearly universal condemnation among both liberal and conservative Puerto Rican leaders of *Roe v. Wade*, the 1973 U.S. Supreme Court decision that made abortion accessible on the mainland, and by law, in Puerto Rico as well. Puerto Rican feminists found themselves the lone voice on the Left in support of the legalization of abortion. Also in 1973, the Puerto Rican legislature enacted Law 57, which created the five-member Commission for Women's Affairs. The commission is charged with improving equity through education and advocacy.

One element that has ignited the feminist movement on the island during the past several decades has been an increasing amount of archeological evidence that suggests that gender equity was a prominent element of indigenous Taíno culture, where women could take on leadership roles as healers and chiefs.

Since the 1980s Puerto Rican feminists have concentrated their efforts on increasing the number of women in political office, an endeavor that reached fruition with the election of Sila Calderón as mayor of San Juan in 1997 and governor in 2001. With more women than men in the workplace, leading feminist activists and scholars continue to focus on improving conditions for working women.

Inspired by the feminist and anti-war movements, gay activists became a more visible component of Puerto Rico's political landscape in 1974, when a group of gay men and lesbians formed the Gay Pride Community. Their work was especially challenging in a highly religious society where homosexuality was prohibited by law until 2003.

NATIONALISM AND PUERTO RICAN PRIDE

The social unrest of the 1960s and 1970s led to a newly energized and radicalized independence movement on the island and in the United States. The most radical and militant activities emanated from two organizations: the island-based *Ejército Popular Boricua-Macheteros* (Boricua Popular Army) and Chicago's *Fuerzas Armadas de Liberación Nacional* or Armed Forces of National Liberation (ALN). Both organizations carried out bombings and armed attacks against military, government, and corporate targets resulting in the deaths of police, military personnel, and some civilians. After a long investigation the Federal Bureau of Investigation arrested twenty-five members of both militant organizations in Puerto Rico and throughout the United States in the 1980s.

Nationalism took less violent and visible forms as well. In New York City and elsewhere, organizations like the Young Lords proclaimed a Puerto Rican identity, protested discrimination against those living in the U.S. *colonias* of New York, Chicago, New Haven, Connecticut, and New Jersey, as well as the exploitation of Puerto Rican workers on the island by industry and the military. Resistance to the Vietnam War played a role in this new activism in the United States and on the island, particularly by those who argued that Puerto Ricans should not have to fight in a war orchestrated by a president and legislative body that they had no say in electing. One notable act of civil disobedience took place in October 1977, when about 25 demonstrators took over the Statue of Liberty in New York City for several hours, hanging a Puerto Rican flag from the statue's crown. Additional protestors gathered below, on the grounds of Battery Park, in support of the Statue of Liberty demonstrators. Spokesmen for both groups said they were seeking independence for Puerto Rico, an end to discrimination against Puerto Ricans, and the release of prisoners serving terms for the 1954 U.S. Congressional shootings.

Another offshoot of this new form of Puerto Rican nationalism was an unprecedented interest among Puerto Rican students on and off the island in their history and heritage. Students in New York City, Chicago, and San Juan demanded the opportunity to enroll in classes in Taíno history, as well as the history of slavery and Afro-Puerto Rican culture, and women's studies. However, traditional Puerto Rican scholarship had ignored many of these areas; some had even declared that there was nothing to study— none of these groups had made a lasting impact on the culture or significantly contributed to the island's history. However, U.S. and Puerto Rican schools agreed to hold the classes students were asking for and funds were soon made available to pursue new research to foster the curriculum. New research funding paved the way for a new generation of feminist, Afro-Puerto Rican, and indigenous studies scholars to comb through previously neglected documents. For example, from the U.S. invasion in 1898 until the mid-1970s, much of the island's four centuries' worth of colonial documents under Spanish rule were housed, but never officially archived, in the basement of the Library of Congress. Due to the efforts of influential historian Arturo Morales Carrión, those documents were turned over to the Puerto Rican government three decades ago and have provided Puerto Rican scholars with a wealth of material that is still being mined, re-discovered, and reinterpreted.

MIGRATION BACKLASH, 1970s–1980s

The work of groups like the Young Lords was spurred in part by a backlash to the large-scale Puerto Rican migration into the United States that began in the 1940s and continued into the 1980s. According to critics, Puerto Ricans could not assimilate into the culture, refused to speak English, and brought with them a culture of poverty. Their concentration in urban centers led to crime, low educational standards, and the spread of disease. U.S. Census data show a different story. Puerto Ricans are mastering English at about the same rate as past immigrant groups, with functional bilingualism attained by the second generation and, typically, a complete loss of Spanish proficiency experienced by the third or fourth generations. In fact, a large number of Puerto Ricans born in the United States speak no Spanish. Puerto Rican students' academic success is correlated to economic status, with some key discrepancies. For example, Puerto Rican students tend to outperform their peers in some academic areas, such as their presence in honors and AP classes. In addition, income levels of Puerto Ricans living in the States increased by 30 percent in the 1980s, more than any other ethnic group. This success was highly correlated to enhanced educational attainment. Teen birth rates and other health factors are also closely aligned with economic status. In other words, poverty, not Puerto Rican identity, is the root cause of gaps in academic and employment achievement and accounts for the figures that have often been employed since the 1970s when social critics first started discussing the "Puerto Rican problem."

On the island some have expressed concern about out-migration. As educational attainment levels stagnated in the 1980s when the government decided to stem its fiscal problems by keeping education funding flat and cutting teachers' salaries, some expressed concern that these policies would intensify a "brain drain" of the island's brightest, most educated, and highest-skilled workers, who would choose to migrate to the States in search of higher paychecks and better educational opportunities. There seems to be little evidence of a "brain drain" phenomenon in migration figures, as Puerto Rican migrants represent a cross-section of the population and their education and professional skills are nearly identical to the overall population. However, some professionals are over-represented in migrant numbers, including nurses and engineers.

TWO MORE PLEBISCITES, 1993 AND 1998

Like Puerto Ricans on and off the island, the U.S. courts have spent several decades trying to determine exactly what Freely Associated State/ Commonwealth status means in the lives of everyday Puerto Ricans and in the island's legal relationship with the United States. In 1980, for example, the U.S. Supreme Court ruled that Congress could treat Puerto Rico differently than a state. In 1987, the First Circuit Court of Appeals stated that Puerto Rico is a sovereign entity, separate from the United States. In 1993, the Eleventh Circuit Court of Appeals seemed to rule the opposite. The Puerto Rican people seem equally confused, or perhaps frustrated, as evidenced in the last two plebiscites.

In 1993 the pro-statehood governor held a plebiscite that rendered mixed results: 48.8 percent voted for "improved" Commonwealth status, 46.2 percent for statehood, and 4.4 percent for independence. With no one option garnering more than 50 percent of the vote, there was no clear consensus among voters for leaders to advocate to Congress. A change toward some irrevocable path, such as independence or statehood, many argued, should not be undertaken until a nearly unanimous agreement was reached.

In 1998, the pro-statehood leaders in power thought they could garner such an agreement on the statehood path. The results of the 1998 plebiscite were even more ambiguous than the 1993 vote: 50.3 percent of voters chose "None of the Above"; 46.5 percent voted for statehood; 2.5 percent for independence; 0.1 percent for Commonwealth status; and 0.3 percent for free association.

Some journalists and political pundits theorized that the mixed results were a way for the electorate to express its frustrations with the New Progressive administration's attempts to privatize public services such as the state-owned telephone company, which had prompted widespread strikes and pro-labor demonstrations in 1997 to 1998.

8

Puerto Rico Today (1999–2009)

NONE OF THE ABOVE

The 1998 Plebiscite offered voters five choices arrayed in the following order: (1) territorial commonwealth, (2) free association, (3) statehood, (4) independence, and (5) none of the above (though none of the preceding would be a better translation of the wording). Over 50 percent of voters opted for choice number 5.

The cultural and political fallout from the 1998 Plebiscite is still the talk of the Puerto Rican community on and off the island. In conversation, many Puerto Ricans proudly claim that this is the option they chose. Political analysts have argued that voting for the option was a way of maintaining the status quo, but it could just as easily be seen as a way of questioning the plebiscite and the officials who administered it. It can also be interpreted as a way for Puerto Rican voters to question the U.S. governmental mechanisms surrounding island governance, including U.S. government officials who had stated prior to the vote that they would do nothing to facilitate statehood if that were the option selected by the majority. In addition, the fifth option, *"ninguna de las anteriores"* does not quite translate as "none of the above" but rather closer to "none of what has come before." Clearly, the pro-statehood politicians who had drafted the wording and presentation of the ballot meant to communicate that this was the choice for those voters who were not satisfied with any of the choices enumerated before, but the voters may have taken this to mean—or chosen to interpret it to mean—none of the political solutions that have come before in the island's history.

A commonly stated phrase among Puerto Ricans is that in his heart every Puerto Rican desires independence but in his brain and for the good of his wallet he wants some form of continued association with the United States. It is a joke, told with a smile, but often it is followed up by a caveat—that the form of association must allow the Puerto Rican to retain his dignity. An increasing number of Puerto Ricans are said to be unhappy with the current state of the government arrangement with the United States; however, at least 90 percent of Puerto Ricans say that any future form of government must allow them to retain U.S. citizenship.

CONTEMPORARY CULTURE

Life expectancy increased from 46 in the 1940s to 75 by 1990 and over 78 in 2009. Infant mortality rates improved and the birth rate has dropped as people are having smaller families and waiting longer to start them. Though the island has seen a substantial increase in the number of high school graduates, the graduation rate was only 50 percent by 1990 and 66 percent in 2006. Just over 20 percent of the population had college degrees by the 1990s, while less than 2 percent were college educated in 1950. Though education has improved, education rates still lag behind more highly developed economies.[1]

In surveys most young Puerto Ricans see themselves as Puerto Rican first and U.S. citizens second. Popular and youth culture share as much, if not more, in common with the cultures of other Caribbean and Latin American populations as they do with U.S. youth or pop culture. This is also true in areas of traditional culture, dance, music, painting, sculpture, poetry and many forms of literature. All of these forms illustrate a pastiche of African, European, Amerindian, Caribbean, and U.S. influences to create a culture that is uniquely contemporary and uniquely Puerto Rican. U.S. cultural influences are most obvious in hip hop and consumer culture, such as fashion and beauty. Even in these forms of endeavor, Puerto Ricans tend to imprint their own identity onto new forms. In turn, Puerto Ricans' inventions and accommodations influence wider consumer culture, from music to fashion to film.

The traditional marker for Puerto Ricanness, Spanish, is evolving, as education levels improve and more young Puerto Ricans are becoming proficient in both Spanish and English. Circular migration (migration back and forth to the United States) has contributed to this bilingualism. It has been argued that the younger generations on the island are almost as likely to employ Spanglish (a combination of English and Spanish via a process sometimes called "code-switching") as Puerto Ricans born and/or raised in the United States. This code-switching between English and Spanish has long been a hallmark of Puerto Rican literature produced in the States, but is now beginning to be seen in music lyrics and literature produced by artists and writers living on the island as well. Many young Puerto Ricans describe themselves as hybrids, negotiating a space between Latin American and Anglo-American cultures, just as past Puerto Rican artists and cultural agents blended Hispanic, African, and Amerindian traditions into a new culture that is uniquely Puerto Rican.

TAÍNO CULTURE

The emergence of evidence supporting the continued influence of the Taíno and Carib cultures in the lives of modern-day Puerto Ricans has created pride as well as controversy. Many Puerto Ricans think of themselves as a mix of cultures and ethnicities—primarily Spanish, African, and Taíno. However, some have argued that Taíno inheritance is minimal and the Puerto Rican tendency to embrace this heritage is a way of negating more probable African ancestry. Conversely, others have argued that negating Taíno-Carib cultural and hereditary presence is a way of attempting to sever Puerto Ricans' connection to their land, their cultural inheritance, and their claims of sovereignty.

There are several regional tribal groups who claim direct lineage to Taíno and Carib ancestors, including several bands, many unrecognized by the government. The United Confederation of Taíno People, which is recognized by the U.S. government, works in association with local Taíno communities on the island as well as some tribal bands that have formed on the mainland, notably in New Jersey. Since 2000, Taíno communities have occasionally had disputes with the government, particularly over the display of human remains at archeological sites that are open to tourists. Tribal bands have also negotiated to maintain continued access to excavation sites, such as ball courts and villages, during research and construction projects so that they can perform rituals that honor their ancestors. Tribal leaders have advocated that U.S. federal legislation guiding American Indian research, such as the Native American Graves Protection and Repatriation Act, be recognized and adhered to by the Puerto Rican government and leading educational and cultural institutions.

Despite such controversies, most Puerto Ricans have welcomed each new discovery made by scholars about the history of the Taíno and their continued cultural relevance, and are hungry to learn more. Reclaiming and celebrating Taíno culture has become an increasingly important part of Puerto Rican identity, with a growing tendency among Puerto Ricans on and off the island to refer to themselves, according to Taíno custom, as Boriquas or Borinquenos.

ECONOMY

Puerto Rico is considered a middle-income country, according to the World Bank. Though manufacturing jobs have migrated to regions with even cheaper labor and fewer protections for workers, the Puerto Rican economy has been bolstered by an informal economy that includes off-the-books labor, social welfare, credit card debt, and crime, which some economists theorize makes up nearly one-third of the income on the island. This informal income makes it possible for Puerto Ricans on the island to continue to fulfill their consumer aspirations. The role of culture consumer has in turn forged identity, particularly in the younger generation. From this perspective, Puerto Ricans have been successfully "Americanized" in that they are, according to many economic indicators, just as addicted to shopping and credit card debt as consumers of all ethnic backgrounds living in the States.

Puerto Ricans on and off the island are still grappling with the legacy of racial stratification that took hold of the country during the nineteenth century. There are large disparities in wealth, with about 50 percent of the population living below the poverty level. The government is the largest employer on the island and the average income is about one-third as high as the average U.S. income and 75 percent of the income earned by Puerto Ricans living in the United States. However, the median standard of living is higher in Puerto Rico than in many other countries in Latin America and the Caribbean.

In the 1940s two-thirds of the island's population lived in rural areas and nearly half of the population worked in agriculture. By the late 1990s two-thirds of the population lived in urban areas and less than 4 percent of the workforce worked in agriculture. Today, more than half the job market is white collar, although one-third of the jobs are contingent—temporary or part-time. Because the population on the island has more than tripled since 1900, unemployment rates would be much higher without continued large-scale migration to the United States. It is estimated that there are as many, if not more Puerto Ricans living in the States than on the island. However, the number may be even greater depending on how one counts "Puerto

Ricans"—those who were born on the island or whose parents were born on the island; if one counts as Puerto Ricans anyone of Puerto Rican descent then the number of "Puerto Ricans" living off the island is higher—about 4 million according to the 2000 Census. The effect of migration to the States has been balanced by migration of Puerto Ricans back to the island. In some cases these in-migrations are native-born Puerto Ricans who stay in the States for two to three years or less, while in other cases Puerto Ricans whose parents or ancestors are from the island are returning to work or retire. This migration pattern is called circular migration, which Puerto Ricans sometimes refer to as *el vaiven* or "the coming and going." In addition, the island has become a destination for immigrants from other countries, especially from the Dominican Republic. Over 9 percent of the population on the island was born in another country.

CIRCULAR MIGRATION AND DIASPORA

Just under 4 million people live on the island, with another 3.4 million Puerto Ricans living in the United States, according to the 2000 U.S. Census. These numbers are not expected to increase significantly by 2010. However, within this population each decade more than 300,000 Puerto Ricans leave the island and settle in the United States, while just over 200,000 have tended to return from the United States to reside on the island. The numbers have varied slightly over the past two decades, but are generally consistent, so that in the 1990s, Puerto Rico experienced a net migration of just over 110,000 with a similar number projected for the years 2000 to 2010.

Puerto Ricans who return to the island after years spent in the United States affect the culture as well as the economy. Though many of these "immigrants" are returning to the island after leaving to work in the United States for years, sometimes decades, others are the descendents of island-born Puerto Ricans. Born in the United States, many have never lived on the island before. These Puerto Ricans bring their cultural influences with them, from Spanglish to music to cuisine.

One of the most prominent examples of the cultural and artistic give-and-take created by Puerto Rico's cross-migration pattern can be found in the realm of music. Though the origins of salsa music are hard to pin down, some of the genre's most prominent and innovative artists have been Puerto Ricans living in the U.S. Diaspora, particularly in New York City. Combining elements of traditional Cuban music and Afro-Puerto Rican *bomba* and *plena* with touches of African American jazz, salsa emerged in the mid-twentieth century as a musical tradition largely engineered in the United States and adopted by Puerto Ricans on the island, where artists added their own touches, which were, in turn, taken up by U.S.-based artists, and so on.

The same pattern has been seen in the evolution of Puerto Rican hip hop, reggaeton, and other contemporary music genres. In fact, it may be misleading to speak of "Puerto Rican hip hop" since the emergence of hip hop and rap in the 1970s came out of New York neighborhoods where African Americans, Puerto Ricans, and Dominicans lived side by side and where Caribbean-imported reggae, particularly the practice of "toasting" or speaking over rhythmic music, had a transformational influence on African American musicians and disc jockeys.

Similar examples of cross-cultural influence can be found in other art forms, such as literature, or in such contemporary cultural phenomenon as fashion.

VIEQUES

On April 19, 1999 a civilian guard, David Sanes, was killed during military exercises held at the U.S. Navy base on Vieques. For years local fishermen and other islanders had protested the presence of the base on the island, and in the wake of Sanes' death, local citizens' protests were soon joined by Puerto Ricans from throughout the island and then by Puerto Ricans in the States. A coalition of groups held rallies, marches, and strikes. Hundreds of civilians built camps on beaches that were property of the Navy. Over the next year, thousands came to visit the camps and show their support for the protesters and the people of Vieques. Residents pointed to a history of health problems that they said were caused by materials used in weapons testing. They demanded that the Navy leave Vieques or at least stop exercises and weapons testing. President Bill Clinton offered a compromise—a referendum on the issue would be held on the island in 2000 and if a majority of the people of Vieques voted for a termination of operations, the Navy would leave by 2003. In the meantime, the protestors would be removed and weapons tests using conventional payloads would be held for only 90 days each year until the base was closed. Though the Puerto Rican government in San Juan agreed to these terms, the demonstrators were not satisfied with the referendum's two options. Protests continued, including large-scale marches in Puerto Rico and the United States—some reaching attendance of up to 150,000 by some estimates—and visits to the campsites by thousands more, including Puerto Rican celebrities like actors Edward James Olmos and Rosie Perez.

In 2003 the Navy halted operations on Vieques and the base was closed in 2004. The U.S. government designated the property formerly owned by the Navy as a natural preserve and the island is now a popular tourist destination, known for its bioluminescent bays (the presence of organisms in the water that appear to glow at night).

PUERTO RICO SUCCUMBS TO THE WORLDWIDE RECESSION

The worldwide recession has had devastating results for Puerto Rico, where economic growth was stagnant in 2006 and the overall economy actually contracted in 2007, 2008, and the beginning of 2009. As the international debt crisis continued to play out in the world financial markets, the island contended with its own debt crisis, which was exacerbated by rising unemployment figures, a government budgetary deficit, and high rates of personal debt, as well as billions of dollars in government debt, all of which led to a sinking bond rating, making it more difficult to find creditors willing to back debt. In response, the island's newly elected New Progressive governor, Luis Guillermo Fortuño-Burset, implemented an austerity package that included large layoffs of government workers, prompting widespread demonstrations. The governor also proposed tax increases and the creation of a new type of government bond that he hoped would attract investors and alleviate the government's interest payments on its debt. As this book was heading to press, Fortuño-Burset seemed to have enticed at least some mutual funds into considering purchase of his bonded debt instrument.[2]

THE PRESIDENT'S TASK FORCE ON PUERTO RICO'S STATUS

In 1992, President George H. W. Bush ordered that all governmental departments should treat Puerto Rico as a state unless doing so would disrupt programs and operations. In 2000 President Clinton established a Task Force to identify options for Puerto Rico's future status. By 2003, President George W. Bush ordered the Task Force to issue reports every two years, the most recent in 2007. The Task Force reiterated previous findings that limited Puerto Rico's options to its current territorial status, statehood, or independence. The analysis of the constitutional options seemed to negate PDP claims that the current Commonwealth status represents a mutually agreed-on governance by mutual consent. However, it seemed to suggest that Puerto Rico could opt for a form of independence, called freely associated statehood that would allow Puerto Ricans to retain their U.S. citizenship and the U.S. military to provide security for the island. Interestingly, despite the use of the term *Estado Libre Asociado* to describe the current Commonwealth status, according to the Task Force report, Puerto Rico is not actually one of the countries that officially has this status. If Puerto Ricans opted for this status, they would need to understand that it is a form of independence and can be terminated unilaterally by the United States at any time.

The Task Force recommended holding a series of plebiscites in the coming years to make sure the options are clear to voters. For example, the first plebiscite would simply ask voters if they did or did not want to continue being governed under the current Commonwealth status. If the voters chose to change their status, the second plebiscite would ask voters to choose between statehood and independence. If they selected independence, then a third plebiscite would allow voters to select from a range of options, including an actual, legally sanctioned freely associated state. Even if voters chose to retain the Commonwealth condition, the Task Force urges the government to continue holding plebiscites periodically until the issue is "solved." Puerto Rico's Resident Commissioner Pedro Pierluisi seemed to be following the recommendations of the Presidential Task Force to the letter when he submitted the Puerto Rico Democracy Act of 2009 (H.R. 2499) to Congress in May 2009. The bill called for a plebiscite that would contain two options for Puerto Rican voters—remaining under the island's present commonwealth status or opting for a follow-up plebiscite with a range of governance options, ranging from statehood to independence. The pro-statehood New Progressive party favors the bill, while the pro-commonwealth and pro-independence parties have voiced opposition to it. In June 2009, the U.S. House Committee on Natural Resources held hearings on the bill with Governor Fortuño and other Puerto Rican leaders as featured speakers. In July, the committee approved the bill and sent it to the U.S. House of Representatives for a full vote. At the time this book was going to press a majority of U.S. Congressmen and Senators reportedly favored the bill.[3]

Notable People in the History of Puerto Rico

Ralph Abercromby (1734–1801)—British general who attempted to capture the island in 1796.

Agueybana (?–1510)—Taíno chief who served as battle commander in the Taíno Uprising of 1510 and was killed in battle before his force's ultimate defeat by Governor Juan Ponce de León.

Pedro Albizu Campos (1893–1965)—Harvard-educated lawyer, World War I veteran, president of the Nationalist party, and the island's most famous independence activist and revolutionary spokesman.

Pope Alexander VI (1431–1503)—Declared that any future discoveries in the New World (the Americas) were Spain's by divine right.

Charles Herbert Allen (1848–1934)—Puerto Rico's first U.S. civilian governor.

José Celso Barbosa (1857–1921)—An Afro-Puerto Rican doctor and founder of the first pro-statehood party after U.S. occupation, whose enthusiasm for the United States was based in large part on his admiration for Abraham Lincoln.

Antonio R. Barceló (1868–1938)—Founder of the Federal party, later the Union and Alliance parties, both of which he led. After a dispute with Luis Muñoz Marín over the nature of Puerto Rico's possible autonomous relationship with the United States, Barceló expelled Muñoz Marín from the Alliance party and Muñoz Marín founded the present-day Popular Democratic Party.

Segundo Ruiz Belvis (1829–1867)—Abolitionist and one of the organizers of the 1868 Grito de Lares uprising.

Ramón E. Betances (1827–1898)—Abolitionist, physician, nationalist, organizer of the 1868 Grito de Lares uprising, and author of the Ten Commandments of Free Men.

John R. Brooke (1838–1926)—U.S. general who in 1898 became Puerto Rico's first governor under U.S. military occupation.

Julia de Burgos (1917–1953)—Puerto Rican poet and independence activist.

José Campeche (1751–1809)—Painter, famous for his religious works and portraiture, particularly of important members of Puerto Rico's eighteenth-century elite.

Bartolomé de las Casas (1484–1566)—Catholic priest famous for describing atrocities committed against the Taíno and Carib people by the Spanish in *A Short Account of the Destruction of the Indies* and other documents.

Ramón de Castro y Gutierrez (Governor from 1795–1804)—Spanish general and governor of Puerto Rico who successfully led an outnumbered force consisting of Spanish soldiers and native volunteers to defend the island against the British forces of General Ralph Abercromby in 1796.

Charles V, the Holy Roman Emperor (1500–1558)—Son of Queen Juana of Castile and grandson of Ferdinand and Isabella I, whose reign united the kingdoms of Aragon and Castile into a geographic entity resembling modern-day Spain and witnessed the expansion of Spain's colonization of the Americas.

Roberto Clemente (1934–1972)—Professional baseball player and humanitarian who died in a plane crash while attempting to deliver medial supplies to Nicaragua.

George Clifford, the Earl of Cumberland (1558–1605)—English admiral who invaded Puerto Rico in 1598.

Roberto Cofresí y Ramírez de Arellano (1791–1825)—Pirate who started out as a Spanish patriot attacking U.S. and British ships, but later favored independence and attacked Spanish ships as well until he was captured and executed.

Christopher Columbus (1451–1506)—Italian explorer voyaged to the Americas under the flag of Castile (one of the kingdoms of Spain); he is often credited with "discovering America." Born Genoese Cristoforo Colombo, he was called Cristóbal Colón by the Spanish.

Diego Columbus (1479/80?–1526)—Son of Christopher Columbus who spent much of his life trying to hold the Spanish monarchs to the agreements that were made with his father, which would have given his family significant control over the Americas. He served as governor of Spain's Caribbean holdings, including Puerto Rico, in the early 1500s and was a political enemy of Puerto Rico's first governor Juan Ponce de León.

Sir Francis Drake (1540–1596)—Considered a pirate by the Spanish and a hero by the English, he attempted to invade Puerto Rico in 1595.

Ferdinand II (1452–1516)—King of Aragon and co-ruler with his wife, Isabel I, of the Iberian nation that would become unified Spain under their grandson Charles. He ruled during the time that Christopher Columbus first encountered Puerto Rico in 1493 and during much of its early colonization.

Luis A. Ferré (1904–2003)—Governor of Puerto Rico from 1969 to 1973 and leader of the pro-statehood New Progressive Party.

Luis Guillermo Fortuño-Burset—Former Resident Commissioner and ninth elected Governor since the establishment of Puerto Rico's Commonwealth status. Since becoming governor in January 2009, Fortuño-Burset, a member of the pro-statehood New Progressive Party, has testified on behalf of the Puerto Rico Democracy Act, a bill in the U.S. House of Representatives that would institute a fourth island-wide plebiscite on Puerto Rico's status, and instituted controversial measures to curb government spending in response to the worldwide credit crisis.

Boudewijn Hendriksz—Dutch commander who attempted to capture Puerto Rico in 1625.

Docoudray Holstein (1763–1839)—A German national who fought in Simón Bolívar's wars to evict Spain from Latin America until the two had a falling out. In 1822 Holstein attempted to lead an elaborate attack on Puerto Rico that he hoped would spur a large-scale uprising and simultaneous slave revolts with the objective of ousting the Spanish. His plot was discovered as he was sailing toward Puerto Rico and he and about 400 fellow would-be revolutionaries, most of them from the United States, were arrested in Curaçao.

Isabella I (1451–1504)—Queen of Castile and co-ruler with her husband Ferdinand II of the Iberian nation that would become unified Spain under their grandson Charles. She ruled during the time that Christopher Columbus first encountered Puerto Rico in 1493.

Juana I (1479–1555)—Queen of Castile, daughter of King Ferdinand and Queen Isabella, she was accused of insanity and spent much of her adult life in a power struggle with her father. Her son Charles, the Holy Roman Emperor, united Aragon and Castile as well as other provinces under his reign, making him the first sovereign to rule over the region typically thought of as "Spain." She is sometimes referred to as "La Loca" or "the mad one."

Manuel Macías y Casado (1845–1937)—Last Spanish governor of Puerto Rico; as general he led the troops that surrendered to the U.S. forces during the Spanish-American War.

William McKinley (1843–1901)—President of the United States during the Spanish-American War.

Nelson Miles (1839–1925)—General who led the U.S. invasion during the Spanish-American War and captured Puerto Rico.

Luis Muñoz Marín (1898–1980)—First democratically elected governor of Puerto Rico, primary author of the constitution that established the island's current commonwealth form of government, founder of the pro-commonwealth Popular Democratic Party, and architect of Operation Bootstrap, the economic program that transformed the island from an agricultural to an industrial economy in the mid-twentieth century.

Luis Muñoz Rivera (1859–1916)—Puerto Rico's most prominent advocate for independence during the waning years of Spanish colonialism and the early years of U.S. occupation.

Alejandro O'Reilly (1722–1794)—Special Envoy of the Spanish King who conducted a detailed census of the island in 1765.

Nicolas de Ovando (1460–1518)—Territorial governor of the Indies (the portion of the Caribbean Islands that had been discovered by the Spanish in the early sixteenth century), known for his brutal treatment of indigenous people, particularly on Hispaniola (modern-day Haiti and the Dominican Republic).

Genara Pagin (?–1963)—A Puerto Rican suffragist and labor activist who worked as a garment worker in New York City. After the 19th Amendment was passed, she traveled to Puerto Rico and attempted to vote in the 1920 election, claiming that if she had the right to vote as a U.S. citizen in the United States, then she should also have the right to vote in the U.S. territory of Puerto Rico. The U.S. Department of Interior ruled that she did not have this right.

Juan de la Pezuela y Caballos (1809–1906)—Spanish governor who issued the 1849 law of *libreta* or *Reglamento de Jornaleros* (Workers' Regulations), which required all farm workers to carry a passbook to prove that they were employed by a large landowner.

Jesús T. Piñero (1897–1952)—First Puerto Rican appointed governor.

Juan Ponce de León (1474–1521)—Puerto Rico's first governor, he was the first European to voyage to Florida, where he was killed by the Calusa people.

Ramón Power y Giralt (1775–1813)—Abolitionist and Puerto Rican delegate to the Spanish Parliament in 1810, he was elected vice president of Parliament and played a substantial role in the composition of the first Spanish Constitution in 1812.

Juan Prim (1814–1870)—Governor of Puerto Rico and author of the Black Code, which encouraged the abusive treatment of slaves and free blacks as well. He later went on to earn fame and multiple titles for his involvement in numerous wars and court intrigues in Spain.

Montgomery Reily (1866–1954)—U.S. civilian governor to Puerto Rico (1921–1923) who the legislature tried to impeach. He declared speech in favor of independence and the bearing of the Puerto Rican flag to be acts of treason because they advocated the overthrow of the U.S. government, reasoning that would be used in the decades to come by later governors to silence dissent.

Francis E. Riggs—Unpopular police commissioner assassinated in 1936; his death resulted in a crackdown on pro-independence activists and island-wide unrest.

Manuel Rojas (1820–?)—One of the leaders of the 1868 Grito de Lares uprising.

Carlos Romero Barceló (1932–)—Two-term governor who is credited with redefining and strengthening the pro-statehood New Progressive Party.

Theodore Roosevelt Jr. (1887–1934)—Popular U.S. civilian governor who tried to raise money from the public and private sector to alleviate Puerto Rico's economic crisis in the early 1930s.

Arturo A. Schomburg (1874–1938)—Born in Puerto Rico, he became a follower of African separatist Marcus Garvey and a member of the Revolutionary Committee of Puerto Rico after moving to New York City. His vast collection of papers and artifacts relating to Africans and members of the African Diaspora became the cornerstone of the archives now kept at the Schomburg Center for Research in Black Culture in Harlem.

Miguel de la Torre (1783–1843)—Governor from 1823 to 1837, whose autocratic style made him unpopular with the Puerto Rican people.

Rexford Guy Tugwell (1891–1979)—Last non-Puerto Rican appointed governor; he formed a partnership with then-president of the legislature Luis Muñoz Marín to make sweeping changes in the island's social and economic institutions.

Urayoán—Taíno chief involved in the ultimately devastating Taíno Uprising of 1510, which killed as many as 200 settlers before its leaders were defeated by Governor Juan Ponce de León.

Blanton Winship (1869–1947)—U.S. civil governor who implemented a strict law-and-order approach to the growing independence and labor activism of the 1930s.

Glossary of Selected Terms

AUTONOMIC CHARTER—An agreement between Spain and Puerto Rico signed in 1897 that was designed to place Puerto Rico on the road toward autonomy. It created a democratically elected legislature, independent judiciary, and the power to negotiate trade agreements and alter the nature of the relationship with Spain at any time, making it far more autonomous by many measures than Puerto Rico's current relationship with the United States.

BANDA CONTRA LA RAZA AFRICANA—Often called the Black Code, Governor Juan Prim created this set of rules in 1848 that decimated the human rights of both slaves and free blacks on the island and indemnified whites in confrontations with Afro-Puerto Ricans. Its stated purpose was to prevent slave uprisings and conspiracies.

BATEY—Court on which the indigenous Taíno people played a game using a rubber ball. This ball game was the centerpiece of inter-community festivals called *areytos*.

BEHIQUE—Taíno (indigenous Puerto Rican) healer or shaman, could be male or a post-menopausal female.

BOHIO—House of Taíno (indigenous Puerto Rican) laborers; a term that is still used to describe a simple rural dwelling in some parts of the island.

BORINQUEN—The name used by the indigenous Taínos for Puerto Rico that is still used (with a multitude of spelling variations) by many contemporary Puerto Ricans when referring to the island. It means "Land of the Noble Lord."

CACICAZGOS—Communities or villages inhabited by the Taíno, the indigenous people of Puerto Rico.

CACIQUE—Taíno (indigenous Puerto Rican) chief, both men and women could hold this title.

CANEY—The house of a Taíno (indigenous Puerto Rican) chief and his or her family.

CARIB—Also called the Kalinago or Island-Carib, this warrior community from South America's Orinoco River basin were at war with the Taíno when the Spaniards arrived in the late 1490s. Later they formed an alliance with the Taíno in an effort to expel the Spanish from Puerto Rico and the rest of the Caribbean.

CASSAVA—This root vegetable, also called manioc or yucca, was the staple food of the Taíno, who inhabited Puerto Rico prior to the arrival of the Spanish.

CÉDULA DE GRACIAS (WARRANT OF OPPORTUNITY)—This 1815 decree granted free land and tax exemptions to new settlers and was designed to encourage immigration to Puerto Rico.

CHARDON PLAN—A plan devised in the mid-1930s by economist Carlos Chardon, Governor Rexford Tugwell, and Luis Muñoz Marín to reorient the Puerto Rican economy away from large industrial farms toward smaller family farms, and to diversify industrial endeavors based on local resources.

COLONIAS—Colonies, used to describe Puerto Rican enclaves in U.S. cities, such as New York, Chicago, and Boston.

CONQUISTADORES—Spanish settlers, literally "conquerors."

CORTES—Spanish parliament.

CRIOLLO—Native-born Puerto Rican. In Spanish this term is also used to refer to anyone born in the Americas. It does not have the same meaning as the word "creole" has in formerly French colonial regions of the Americas.

EJÉRCITO POPULAR BORICUA-MACHETEROS—Militant island-based nationalist organization that orchestrated bombings and other violent forms of resistance in the 1970s.

ENCOMIENDO—A parcel of land given to a Spanish settler by decree of the king or queen.

FORAKER ACT—These guidelines enacted in 1900 by the U.S. Congress replaced U.S. military occupation with a government largely presided over by U.S. civilians appointed by the President, approved by the Congress, with bureaucratic oversight provided by various divisions of the War Department and limited local input provided by a democratically elected lower legislative chamber.

FUERZAS ARMADAS DE LIBERACIÓN NACIONAL **(FALN; ARMED FORCES OF NATIONAL LIBERATION)**—Chicago-based militant pro-independence organization that staged bombings and other forms of violent insurgent activities in the 1970s.

GAG LAW—Adopted in 1947, it prohibited anyone from advocating the violent overthrow of the U.S. government by arguing for Puerto Rican independence or displaying a Puerto Rican flag.

GRITO DE LARES—Translated as the "shout at Lares," was an uprising in 1868 in which approximately 600 men and women took up arms against the Spanish colonial government in the town of Lares and declared Puerto Rico a republic.

GUANAHATABEYES—A pre-ceramic people who inhabited Puerto Rico about 4,000 years ago; their descendents were still living in the Caribbean Islands when the Spanish arrived, nearly 3,500 years after their first appearance in the region.

HIDALGOS—Low-ranking Spanish nobles who made up the bulk of the early settlers to Puerto Rico and other Spanish colonies in the Americas.

IBERIAN PENINSULA—The section of Europe currently comprised of the nations of Portugal and Spain.

IGNERI—An indigenous Caribbean people, who made up the majority of the brides captured by the mobile Carib warrior culture prior to the arrival of the Spanish. The women and children of the remaining Carib tribes still speak the Igneri language, which is believed to be closely related to the Taíno.

INSTITUTO CULTURA DE PUERTORRIQUEÑA—Institute created to focus on the Spanish, Taíno, and African heritage of the Puerto Rican people in 1955; its first director was historian Ricardo E. Alegría, famous for his study of the Taíno.

JÍBARO—Mountain peasant or farm worker; a national symbol of pride once used by the Popular Democratic Party as its emblem.

JONES ACT—This set of provisions enacted by Congress in 1916 expanded on the Foraker Act, allowing Puerto Rico slightly more control over local government and granting U.S. citizenship to its inhabitants.

LAW OF *LIBRETA*—Popular name for the Reglamento de Jornaleros (Workers' Regulations) that required all rural residents who did not have large amounts of property to work for wealthier landowners and to carry a passbook with them at all times to prove that they were employed.

LAWS OF THE BURGOS—Queen Juana of Castile announced this set of rules in 1512. Designed to curb the brutal treatment of the indigenous peoples of the Americas by the Spanish, they were largely ignored.

MESTIZO—Term typically referring to someone of European and Amerindian ancestry; this Spanish adjective is also sometimes used to describe persons of any and all mixed-race heritage.

MONA PASSAGE—Portion of the Caribbean Ocean separating Puerto Rico and Hispaniola (modern-day Haiti and the Dominican Republic).

MULATO—Someone of European and African or sometimes Amerindian and African ancestry; it does not necessarily have the same negative connotations that the word "mulatto" has in English.

NABORÍAS—Labor class of the Taíno, the indigenous people of Puerto Rico.

NATIONALIST INSURRECTION OF 1950—A series of violent uprisings intended to disrupt the formation of the *Estado Libre Asociado* (Commonwealth) by pro-independence activists, including assassination attempts on Governor Luis Muñoz Marín, President Harry Truman, and attacks on at least seven Puerto Rican towns.

NEW PROGRESSIVE PARTY *(PARTIDO NUEVO PROGRESISTA* OR PNP)—Pro-statehood party that has rivaled the Popular Democratic Party in popularity since the late 1960s.

NITAÍNOS—Ruling class of the TaÓno, the indigenous people of Puerto Rico.

NUYORICAN—Members of the Puerto Rican Diaspora who live in or near New York City. Coined by poets and activists in the El Barrio section of New York in the 1960s and 1970s and used with pride by those who fit this cultural definition; it is also sometimes used with some derision as a term to refer to all U.S. Puerto Ricans by Puerto Ricans living on the island, though most often there is an element of humor and/or affection intended.

OPERATION BOOTSTRAP (*OPERACIÓN MANOS A LAS OBRA*)—Policy implemented by Governor Muñoz Marín and the Popular Democratic Party to attract foreign industrial investment in the island.

PENINSULARES—Spanish-born settlers to Puerto Rico, particularly those who arrived in the nineteenth century. The term was also sometimes applied to any recent immigrants from Europe or the British Islands.

PLEBISCITE—Referendums on Puerto Rico's status that typically offer voters a choice between statehood, independence, and some form of mutual association or Commonwealth status; there have been three since 1967, all of them calling for Commonwealth status or some unspecified option not expressly articulated.

PONCE MASSACRE—Shooting incident at a planned 1937 Nationalist (pro-independence) Party march in Ponce that resulted in 19 deaths and 100 people wounded.

POPULAR DEMOCRATIC PARTY (PDP IN ENGLISH, *PARTIDO POPULAR DEMOCRÁTICO* OR PPD IN SPANISH)—Founded by Puerto Rico's first democratically elected governor, Luis Muñoz Marín this party presided over the formulation of the island's Constitution and formulated its present governance system, the *Estado Libre Asociado* (Freely Associated State or Commonwealth).

PUERTO RICAN INDEPENDENCE PARTY (*PARTIDO INDEPENDENTISTA PUERTORRIQUEÑO* OR PIP)—Officially approved independence party that has garnered few votes in island-wide elections; does not include outlawed parties and organizations that favor independence.

PRE-CONTACT—The era prior to the arrival of Europeans in the Americas.

PUERTO RICO EMERGENCY RELIEF ADMINISTRATION (PRERA)—An initiative aimed at rebuilding the Puerto Rican economy; it was a component of President Franklin Roosevelt's New Deal.

***REGLAMENTO DE ESCLAVOS* (SLAVE REGULATIONS)**—The first set of regulations in 1789 was designed to protect slaves from the brutality of owners, while the second set of regulations, decreed in 1826 by autocratic Governor Miguel de la Torre, was designed to encourage slave owners to use austere tactics, including brutal corporal punishment, to prevent slave revolts.

***REPARTIMIENDO*—Isabella I of Castile first ordered this apportionment or distribution of the Taíno into divisions of labor. These groups of Taíno laborers were expected to work in an assigned mine or farm for part of the year and be given time to harvest food for their own families the rest the year; it was a system that was abused or ignored by most of the Spanish settlers.

RESIDENT COMMISSIONER—The Foraker Act in 1900 created this post; the Resident Commissioner is elected by the people of Puerto Rico to articulate their concerns to U.S. government officials. In 1904, the role of the Resident Commissioner was expanded making the office holders non-voting member of the U.S. House of Representatives, which is the post's current status.

SALADOID—A group of people, probably from South America, famous for their skill in ceramics who settled in Puerto Rico about 2,500 years ago; they are sometimes referred to as the Hacienda Grande people.

SAN JUAN BAUTISTA—The original Spanish name for Puerto Rico.

SITUADO—Subsidy supplied to colonial Puerto Rico by Spain to pay for the island's fortifications and soldiers' salaries.

SPANISH-AMERICAN WAR—From April to December 1898 the United States carried out a swift defeat of Spanish troops that ended in Spain retreating from Cuba and ceding Puerto Rico, Guam, and the Philippines to the United States.

SPANISH MAIN—Spain's holdings in the Americas during the Age of Exploration, including Puerto Rico as well as most of South America, Central America, the Caribbean, Mexico, and parts of the United States.

STIPULATIONS OF SANTA FE—Promises made to Christopher Columbus at the court of Santa Fe by King Ferdinand and Queen Isabella. Had they been followed, Columbus' descendents would have governed over North, South, and Central America and the Caribbean in perpetuity and controlled 10 percent of its wealth.

TAÍNO—Indigenous people of Puerto Rico, whose complex system of government, religion, and culture dominated much of the Greater and Lesser Antilles prior to the arrival of the Spanish in 1493. In the Taíno language, it literally means "the good people."

TAÍNO UPRISING OF 1510—Sometimes called the Taíno-Carib Uprising, this series of battles led by an alliance of Taíno chiefs that included Aguecbana and Urayoán resulted in the deaths of as many as 200 Spanish settlers before it was thwarted by Governor Juan Ponce de León. Some of the surviving warriors joined their former Carib enemies and waged periodic battles against the Spanish from 1510 to 1513.

TEN COMMANDMENTS OF FREE MEN—Manifesto of liberation enumerating the rights that free people must be given by a just government. According to their author, revolutionary Ramón E. Betances, if these rights do not exist then the people have the right to take up arms against their government.

VIEQUES—Island that was home to a U.S. Navy base until a military exercise killed a civilian guard in 1999 and set off more than a year of protests, forcing the United States to close the Navy base in 2004.

ZEMIS—Carved likenesses of Taíno and Carib gods, also called *cemis*, which are also characteristic of other Arawak peoples.

Notes

PREFACE

1. Kathleen Deagan, "Reconsidering Taíno Social Dynamics after Spanish Conquest: Gender and Class in Culture Contact Studies." *American Antiquity*, Vol. 69, No. 4 (Oct. 2004), pp. 597–626.

CHAPTER 2

1. Arguments and interpretations by contemporary archeologists and ethnohistorians whose work is still evolving both in support of and in contradiction to the mid- to late twentieth-century work of Rouse, Alegría, and others can be found in *Ancient Borinquen: Archeology and Ethnohistory of Native Puerto Rico*, Peter E. Siegel (ed.) (Tuscaloosa: The University of Alabama Press, 2005). For more on debates involving the pre-ceramic to Saladoid transition, please see the Bibliographic Essay.

2. As with the emergence of the Saladoid people, the emergence of the Taíno as a separate culture is another area of dispute among archeologists and ethnohistorians. More information about the leading theories—that the Taínos were direct descendents of the Saladoid people, that they represented an influx of new immigrants from the northeastern coast of South

America, that they represented an influx of immigrants and/or cultural influence from Mesoamerican cultures such as the Maya, or that they were the culmination of a combination of influences—can be found in *Ancient Borinquen: Archeology and Ethnohistory of Native Puerto Rico*, Peter E. Siegel (ed.) (Tuscaloosa, AL: The University of Alabama Press, 2005); *The Indigenous People of the Caribbean*, Samuel M. Wilson (ed.) (Gainesville, FL: University Press of Florida, 1997); and Irving Rouse, *The Taínos: The Rise and Decline of the People who Greeted Columbus* (New Haven, CT: Yale University Press, 1992).

3. More on the matrilineal nature of the Taínos' political and religious hierarchy, as well as on the importance of the feminine deity Attabeira, can be found in *Ancient Borinquen: Archeology and Ethnohistory of Native Puerto Rico*, Peter E. Siegel (ed.) (Tuscaloosa, AL: The University of Alabama Press, 2005). See particularly the chapters "An Introduction to Taíno Culture and History" by Ricardo E. Alegría and "Just Wasting: Taíno Shaman and Concepts of Fertility" by Peter G. Roe.

4. Irving Rouse provides a well-argued defense of the Carib culture in *The Taínos: The Rise and Decline of the People Who Greeted Columbus* (New Haven, CT: Yale University Press, 1992). Another account of Carib culture prior to and just after Contact is provided in "The Caribs of the Lesser Antilles," by Louis Allaire in *The Indigenous People of the Caribbean*, Samuel M. Wilson (ed.) (Gainesville, FL: University Press of Florida, 1997).

5. Juan Carlos Martínez Cruzado, "The Use of Mitochondrial DNA to Discover Pre-Columbian Migrations to the Caribbean: Results for Puerto Rico and Expectations for the Dominican Republic," *Kacike: Journal of Caribbean Amerindian History and Anthropology*, Vol. 3, No.1 (2002), pp. 37–47.

6. Kathleen Deagan, "Reconsidering Taíno Social Dynamics after Spanish Conquest: Gender and Class in Culture Contact Studies," *American Antiquity*, Vol. 69, No. 4 (Oct. 2004), pp. 597–626.

CHAPTER 3

1. Contemporary biographies of Queen Juana, written for scholarly and general audiences, in English and Spanish, have tended to examine the role gender and inter-family rivalries may have played in her depiction as "mad." Nevertheless, many educated in traditional Latin American schoolrooms might have a hard time shaking the colorful archetypal image of "Juana La Loca" from their recollections of history class.

2. Robert H. Fuson, *Juan Ponce de León and the Spanish Discovery of Puerto Rico and Florida* (Blacksburg, VA: McDonald and Woodward Publishing Company, 2000).

3. J.R. McNeill, "Foreword." In *The Columbian Exchange: Biological and Cultural Consequences of 1492: 30th Anniversary Edition*, Alfred W. Crosby, Jr. (Westport, CT: Praeger Publishers, 2003).

4. See Fernando Pico, "Commercial Traffic between Puerto Rico and Seville, 1512–1699, by Number of Ships and Known Tonnage," in *History of Puerto Rico: A Panorama of Its People* (Princeton, NJ: Markus Wiener Publishers, 2005).

CHAPTER 4

1. Olga Jiménez De Wagenheim, *Puerto Rico: An Interpretive History from Pre-Columbian Times to 1900* (Princeton, NJ: Markus Wiener Publishers), p. 137.

2. Economist Andrés Sánchez Tarniella (trans.) in James L. Dietz, *Economic History of Puerto Rico: Institutional Change and Capitalist Development* (Princeton, NJ: Princeton University Press, 1986), p. 12.

3. Eileen J. Suarez-Findlay, *Imposing Decency: The Politics of Sexuality and Race in Puerto Rico: 1870–1930* (Durham, NC: Duke University Press, 1999).

CHAPTER 5

1. James L. Dietz, *Economic History of Puerto Rico: Institutional Change and Capitalist Development* (Princeton, NJ: Princeton University Press, 1986), p. 129.

CHAPTER 7

1. World Travel and Tourism Council, Country Reports, Puerto Rico www.wttc.org

CHAPTER 8

1. Most economic, education, and health statistics in this chapter are from the U.S. Census Bureau, CIA World Factbook https://www.cia.gov/library/publications/the-world-factbook/geos/rq.html, and Francisco Rivera-Batiz and Carlos Enrique Santiago's *Island Paradox: Puerto Rico in the 1990s* (Russell Sage Foundation, 1997).

2. Stan Rosenberg, "Puerto Rico to Sell Debt: Issue of $4.5 Billion Is via Better-Rated Tax Agency," *Wall Street Journal*, June 10, 2009, http://online.wsj.com/article/SB124459322396500275.html.

3. Govtrack.us, http://www.govtrack.us/congress/bill.xpd?bill=h111-2499

Bibliographic Essay

TEXTS AVAILABLE IN ENGLISH

Perhaps the most pleasurable read in English on Puerto Rico is *Puerto Rico in the American Century: A History Since 1898* (Chapel Hill: University of North Carolina Press, 2007) by Cesar J. Ayala and Rafael Bernabe. This book synthesizes the work of other contemporary historians; uncovers new primary source material; examines events from economic, political, social, cultural, and multicultural perspectives; and weaves in illuminating anecdotes and references to Puerto Rican literature, all in clearly written, at times nearly poetic prose that turns a century of history into a riveting, still-unfolding saga. Its rigorous scholarship, accessible style, and extensive bibliography make it an ideal source for students and researchers interested in Puerto Rico's history as a U.S. territory and commonwealth.

There are several good standard histories of the island written in English for a general audience. I found *History of Puerto Rico: A Panorama of Its People* (Princeton, NJ: Markus Wiener Publishers, 2006) by Fernando Pico and *An Economic History of Puerto Rico: Institutional Change and Capitalist Development* (Princeton: Princeton University Press, 1986) by James L. Dietz comprehensive and accessible. *Puerto Rico Past and Present: An Encyclopedia*

(Westport, CT: Greenwood Press, 1998) by Ronald Fernandez and Serafin Mendez Mendez, and Gail Cueto is a useful reference work.

Olga Jiménez de Wagenheim has written many books on Puerto Rico (as has her husband, Kal Wagenheim). Together, the couple authored the document collection, *The Puerto Ricans: A Documentary History* (Princeton, NJ: Markus Wiener Publishers, 2002), a useful source for students looking to incorporate primary sources into their research. Her *Puerto Rico: An Interpretive History from Precolumbian Times to 1900* (Princeton, NJ: Markus Wiener Publishers, 1997) is an extremely useful and accessible guide to Puerto Rican history from Pre-Contact through the nineteenth century, and her concise volume, *Puerto Rico's Revolt for Independence: El Grito de Lares* (Princeton, NJ: Markus Wiener Publishers, 1993), offers a book-length examination of Puerto Rico's only significant armed uprising.

Puerto Rico: A Political and Cultural History, edited by Arturo Morales Carrión (New York: W.W. Norton, 1983), is highly regarded and included in most bibliographies on Puerto Rico, but students should be aware that some material is dated and the book's writing style may seem slightly old-fashioned. Nevertheless, its chapters are exhaustive and well-researched. This collaboration between six of the era's most distinguished Puerto Rican scholars is doubly valuable because the project's lead author was also a public servant. As a special advisor to the Organization of American States' secretary general and as a deputy assistant secretary of state, Morales Carrión helped to shape the political and social policy he and his colleagues write about. Viewed in this context, the book almost serves two purposes: as sound social history testifying to what was known at the time of its printing and as a primary document relating the views of one of the era's most prominent public servants and some of the 1980s most illustrious faculty members from the University of Puerto Rico.

Important work on the history of the indigenous people of Puerto Rico has been conducted by many archeologists and ethnohistorians, particularly in the final decades of the twentieth century. Though much of this work involved researchers from the University of Puerto Rico, nearly all of it is available in English. Some important articles in the field include Ricardo E. Alegría's "On Puerto Rican Archaeology," *American Antiquity*, Vol. 31, No. 2, Part 1 (Oct. 1965), pp. 246–249; Kathleen Deagan's "Reconsidering Taíno Social Dynamics after Spanish Conquest: Gender and Class in Culture Contact Studies," *American Antiquity*, Vol. 69, No. 4 (Oct. 2004), pp. 597–626; and "The Use of Mitochondrial DNA to Discover Pre-Columbian Migrations to the Caribbean: Results for Puerto Rico and Expectations for the Dominican Republic," by Juan Carlos Martínez Cruzado, *Kacike: Journal of Caribbean Amerindian History and Anthropology*, Vol. 3, No. 1 (2002), pp. 37–47.

Ancient Borinquen: Archeology and Ethnohistory of Native Puerto Rico, edited by Peter E. Siegel (Tuscaloosa: The University of Alabama Press, 2005), mostly consists of reports from individual archeological projects undertaken from the late twentieth century to the present. Although reports from the various archeological sites are detailed and specific, the collection is largely free of jargon and accessible to non-specialist readers. Readers looking for more context and connections between archeological discoveries should start with *Taíno: Pre-Columbian Art and Culture from the Caribbean,* edited by Fatima Bercht, Estrellita Brodsky, John Alan Farmer, and Dicey Taylor (New York: The Monacelli Press and El Museo del Barrio, 1997), which contains a wealth of attractive photographs of a large exhibit of Taíno artifacts held in the late 1990s at El Museo del Barrio in New York City. The text consists of chapters on various aspects of Taíno culture written by some of the top scholars in the field, many whose work is not readily available in English, including Ricardo E. Alegría and Marcio Veloz Maggiolo.

The Indigenous People of the Caribbean, edited by Samuel M. Wilson (Gainsville: University Press of Florida, 1997), also contains contributions from some of the most prominent late twentieth-century archeologists, including Louis Allaire, William F. Keegan, and José R. Oliver. The book is the result of the Virgin Islands Humanities Council's response to the 500th anniversary of Columbus' First Voyage. The Council held a series of symposia examining the indigenous peoples of the Caribbean and the legacy of Columbus' voyages to the Americas

The Tainos: Rise and Decline of the People Who Greeted Columbus by Irving Rouse (New Haven: Yale University Press, 1992) offers a comprehensive look at all the indigenous people of Puerto Rico culminating with the Taíno. Rouse, along with Ricardo Alegría, was a pioneer in pre-Columbian Caribbean archeology

There are many Spanish explorers' accounts of the Taíno written during the period of exploration and early colonization, which are considered classics of Hispanic literature and history. *An Account of the Antiquities of the Indians* by Fray Ramón Pane was originally written in 1497, and there are several editions in Spanish. English editions include *A New Edition, with an Introductory Study, Notes, and Appendices* by José Juan Arrom (Durham: Duke University Press, 2000). *Historia de las Indias* (*The History of the Indies*) by Bartolomé de Las Casas, written circa 1525, has numerous volumes, including *An Apologetic History of the Indies.* De Las Casas' *A Short Account of the Destruction of the Indies,* translated by Nigel Griffin, is available from Penguin Classics (New York: 1992, rev. ed. with chronology, 2004). Other accounts include *Historia Natural y General de las Indias* by Gonzalo Fernández de Oviedo y

Valdés and *Historia del Almirante* by Ferdinand Columbus (c. 1539). *Historia Geográfica, Civil y Natural de la Isla de San Juan Bautista de Puerto Rico* by Fray Íñigo Abbad y Lasierra, considered the first real history of the island, was written by a Benedictine monk in 1788. Excerpts of many of these texts can be found in English in various compilations of Caribbean or Hispanic literature. Many of these classic texts are likely to be digitized and placed on the Internet through free Web sites in the coming years as there are no copyright issues. Contemporary translations would still be covered by copyright and most are not widely available in recent English editions, although older translations may be available in some libraries.

More information on the kingdoms of Spain during the discovery and early colonization of Puerto Rico can be found in *Medieval Iberia: An Encyclopedia*, by E. Michael Gerli (New York: Routledge, 2002). Among the many recent re-examinations of Queen Juana of Castile (called Juana La Loca or the Mad One in her day), are *Juana the Mad: Sovereignty and Dynasty in Renaissance Europe*, by Bethany Aram (Baltimore: Johns Hopkins University Press, 2005) and *Juana of Castile: History and Myth of the Mad Queen*, edited by Maria A. Gomez, Santiago Juan-Navarro, and Phyllis Zatlin (Lewisburg, PA: Bucknell University Press, 2008).

Juan Ponce De León and the Spanish Discovery of Puerto Rico and Florida (Blacksburg, VA: McDonald and Woodward Publishing Company, 2000), written by translator and maritime scholar Robert H. Fuson, attempts to rehabilitate Ponce de León's reputation through the extensive use of historic documents from the early colonial period, particularly correspondence between the *conquistadores* and King Ferdinand. Though his language is argumentative, often relying on the extensive employment of exclamations to make his case with a tendency to rely on documents as facts without examining the political context that might surround or influence letter writers and chroniclers from the colonial era, the book is an interesting exercise and a fascinating read. Students should be cautious of the author's tendency to employ speculation and his reluctance to present viewpoints that would tend to refute his argument on Ponce de León's behalf. Still, it is accessible and includes many interesting details from previously untranslated Spanish records. The details of Ponce de León's life are riveting and Fuson makes a lively case on his subject's behalf.

The Columbian Exchange: Biological and Cultural Consequences of 1492, 30th Anniversary Edition, by Alfred W. Crosby, Jr. (Westport, CT: Praeger Publishers, 2003), caused an uproar when it first appeared, changed the course of debate in several fields of study, and still manages to provoke new ways of thinking about colonialism more than 30 years after it was first published. Students should keep in mind that recent scientific studies, most notably on the Taíno and Carib cultures and particularly new evidence of their agricultural practices, have replaced some the theories offered in the book. Nevertheless, Crosby's examination of the biological consequences of 1492 and the subsequent interactions between Europeans, Africans, and indigenous Americans bridges the fields of history, epidemiology, agriculture, and ecology. Students looking for up-to-date information on the ecology of the Caribbean should look elsewhere, but those interested in the history of debate in the fields of biological history and indigenous American history will find this a useful resource and an entertaining read.

The examination of race within the context of Puerto Rican history is an area of vibrant scholarship among contemporary scholars. Most books in this field examine issues of race, particularly the lives of slaves and free black wageworkers in specific municipalities or even on individual plantations. As more documents on the slave trade, post-emancipation working conditions, and the free black communities become available there are likely to be broader-ranging, less specialized titles available for students and general readers. For now, students can get an idea of what life was like for Afro-Puerto Ricans through such titles as Guillermo A. Baralt's *Slave Revolts in Puerto Rico* (1982; Princeton, NJ: Markus Wiener Publishers, 2007 for English translation). Bilingual students may want to skip the awkward translation and seek the original Spanish text.

Regional studies include *Sugar, Slavery, and Freedom in Nineteenth Century Puerto Rico* by Luis A. Figueroa (Chapel Hill: University of North Carolina Press, 2005), a useful and detailed study of slave and post-emancipation labor in Guyama; *Imposing Decency: The Politics of Sexuality and Race in Puerto Rico: 1870–1930* (Durham: Duke University Press, 1999), by Eileen J. Suarez-Findlay, a well-written study of conditions faced by free women of color in Ponce in the generation after the abolition of slavery; and *Sugar and Slavery in Puerto Rico: The Plantation Economy of Ponce, 1800–1850* by Francisco A. Scarano (Madison: University of Wisconsin Press, 1984). Cesár J. Ayala's well-regarded *American Sugar Kingdom: The Plantation Economy of the Spanish Caribbean, 1898–1934* (Chapel Hill: University of North Carolina Press, 1999) examines the plantation economies of Puerto Rico, Cuba, and the Dominican Republic in the early twentieth century.

Puerto Rico: The Four Storyed Country, by José Luis González (Princeton, NJ: Marcus Weiner Publishers, 1993), first written in 1980, examines the legacy of racial tensions on the island. More of a philosophic approach than a historical look at race, Gonzalez's theories on race and class have influenced generations of Puerto Rican historians, political scientists, race theorists, and social scientists, many of whom have followed up with research that contradicts Gonzalez's more general claims.

Neglected by Spain after Mexico, Peru, and wealthier sources of gold and silver were discovered in the Americas, Puerto Rico depended on pirate ships to transport their goods to overseas markets and for needed food and supplies. Many recent books celebrate the Golden Age of Caribbean Piracy as a precursor to democratic rebellion, claiming that piracy was an egalitarian response to the monarchies of the Old World and the brutal hierarchies that existed on most naval ships and privately owned merchant vessels of the time. Among the books in this category are *The Republic of Pirates: Being the True and Surprising Story of the Caribbean Pirates and the Man Who Brought Them Down*, by Colin Woodard (Orlando, FL: Harcourt, 2007) and *Villains of All Nations: Atlantic Pirates in the Golden Age*, by Marcus Rediker (Boston: Beacon Press, 2004). *Pillaging the Empire: Piracy in the Americas 1500–1750*, by Kris E. Lane (Armonk, NY: M.E. Sharpe, 1998), part of Sharpe's Latin American Realities series, examines piracy from the perspective of the Spanish colonists who were often the victims of the trade.

Students looking for a basic, complete account of the Spanish-American War from the perspective of military history will find an accessible read in *The Spanish-American War* by Kenneth E. Hendrickson, Jr. (Westport, CT: Greenwood Press, 2003). Fernando Pico's *Puerto Rico 1898: The War After the War* (1987, translated into English by Sylvia Korwek [Princeton, NJ: Markus Wiener Publishers, 2004]) looks at the two-year military occupation that followed the U.S. invasion through military correspondence, newspaper accounts, and legal documents. A range of well-known scholars look at the political aftermath of the Spanish-American War and U.S. expansionism in *Colonial Crucible: Empire in the Making of the Modern American State*, edited by Alfred W. McCoy and Francisco A. Scarano (Madison, WI: The University of Wisconsin Press, 2009). This volume's essays look at the Philippines, Cuba, and other former and current U.S. territories in addition to Puerto Rico. Among the many books that look at Puerto Rico under U.S. rule and the transition to Commonwealth status are *Puerto Rico: The Trials of the Oldest Colony in the World*, by José Trías Monge (New Haven: Yale University Press, 1997) and *The Disenchanted Island: Puerto Rico and the United States in the Twentieth Century*, by Ronald Fernandez (Westport, CT: Praeger Publishers, 1996), both of which are well-researched, detailed, and present convincing arguments for re-examining Puerto Rico's current political status. Sherrie L. Baver's *The Political Economy of Colonialism: The State and Industrialization in Puerto Rico* (Westport, CT: Praeger, 1993) covers similar ground from a more intensely economic perspective and with a more academic tone. *Toward a Discourse of Consent: Mass Mobilization and Colonial Politics in Puerto Rico, 1932–1948* (Westport, CT: Praeger, 2004) by Gabriel Villaronga is similarly academic in tone and concentrates on the era that marked rapid political change on the island in anticipation of the transition from the Foraker-Jones era to Commonwealth status. A variety of top scholars (many whose scholarship is not otherwise available in English) weigh in on Puerto Rico's status issue in *Colonial Dilemma: Critical Perspectives on Contemporary Puerto Rico*, edited by Edwin Meléndez and Edgardo Meléndez (Cambridge, MA: South End Press, 1993).

Matters of Choice: Puerto Rican Women's Struggle for Reproductive Freedom, by Iris Lopez (Piscataway, NJ: Rutgers University Press, 2008) examines the legacy of birth control and sterilization policies in Puerto Rico, drawing on 25 years of research on sterilized women from five families in Brooklyn.

An interesting document from Puerto Rico's industrialization period is *The Stricken Land: The Story of Puerto Rico*, a memoir and harsh critique of U.S. policy toward Puerto Rico written by the island's last non-Puerto Rican governor, Rexford Guy Tugwell (Charlottesville, VA: University of Virginia Press, 1946).

Legal scholar Efren Rivera Ramos presents a detailed account of Puerto Rico's status issue from 1898 to the present in *American Colonialism in Puerto Rico: The Judicial and Social Legacy* (Princeton, NJ: Markus Wiener Publishers, 2007, revised from a paper presented by the author in 2001). University of Puerto Rico professor Edgardo Meléndez's text, *Puerto Rico's Statehood Movement* (Westport, CT: Greenwood Press, 1988), based on his doctoral dissertation, is still considered a classic, comprehensive look at the origins of the contemporary statehood movement.

For students interested in historiography, *Puerto Rico: A Socio-Historic Interpretation*, by Manuel Maldonado-Denis (New York: Random House, 1972) provides an interesting look at the rhetoric of ethnic studies and history in the 1970s. The author calls his work an "essay" and the entire book can be seen as an argument for independence within the context of the late 1960s and early 1970s. From that perspective it has interesting things to say about class, race, and the island's colonial social inheritance. Interestingly, Maldonado-Denis is dismissive of the Taíno culture.

Economists Francisco L. Rivera-Batiz and Carlos E. Santiago provide detailed analysis of U.S. Census data from the 1950s to 1990s in *Island Paradox: Puerto Rico in the 1990s* (New York: Russell Sage Foundation, 1997). Also in the 1990s, Nancy Morris conducted focus groups with Puerto Rican leaders as well as everyday voters on a range of topics, including political status, and presented the findings in the accessible, jargon-free *Puerto Rico: Culture, Politics, and Identity* (Westport, CT: Praeger Publishers, 1995).

None of the Above: Puerto Ricans in the Global Era, edited by Frances Negrón-Muntaner (New York: Palgrave Macmillan, 2007), is a compilation of essays from a series of symposia hosted by the editor between 2000 and 2004. These academic papers tend to be more focused on cultural issues than the 1998 Plebiscite results. However, for those interested in the status question, two essays make bold cases for and against the need to solve the issue: "'None of the Above' Means More of the Same: Why Solving

Puerto Rico's Status Problem Matters" by Christine Duffy Burnett and "The Political Status of Puerto Rico: A Nonsense Dilemma" by Carlos Pabón. Other chapters examine contemporary identity issues, with a focus on youth culture.

Students interested in the protests on Vieques in the late 1990s and early 2000s will find a book-length treatment in *Military Power and Popular Protest: The U.S. Navy in Vieques, Puerto Rico* by Katherine T. McCaffrey (Piscataway, NJ: Rutgers University Press, 2002).

Though the current volume only mentions the Puerto Rican Diaspora in the United States briefly in contexts where the U.S. Puerto Rican community most directly affected events on the island, it should be remembered that Puerto Ricans have been living in the United States since well before the Spanish-American War. There are many texts on this topic, including *The Puerto Rican Diaspora: Historical Perspectives*, edited by Carmen Teresa Whalen and Victor Vázquez-Hernández (Philadelphia: Temple University Press, 2005), *Puerto Ricans in the United States: A Contemporary Portrait* by Edna Acosta-Belén and Carlos E. Santiago (Boulder, CO: Lynne Rienner Publishers, 2006), *Puerto Rican Voices in English: Interviews with Writers*, by Carmen Dolores Hernández (Westport, CT: Praeger Publishers, 1997), and *From Colonia to Community: The History of Puerto Ricans in New York City, 1917–1948*, by Virginia Sanchez Korrol (Westport, CT: Greenwood Press, 1983).

Among the many government documents available on Puerto Rico is *Puerto Rico: A Guide to the Island of Boriquén*, part of the Federal Writers Project (1940), much of which is now accessible online. Also available as a PDF is *Report by the President's Task Force on Puerto Rico's Status*, December 2007, http://www.usdoj.gov/opa/documents/2007-report-by-the-president-task-force-on-puerto-rico-status.pdf.

TEXTS AVAILABLE IN SPANISH

Those looking for historical information about Puerto Rico will find their task easier if they can read Spanish. *Puerto Rico: Cinco Siglos de Historia, third edition* (Bogotá: McGraw Hill Interamericana, 2008) by Francisco Scarano is a well-respected general history, which has been used for years as the most popular standard textbook in many high school and college history classes on the island. As of this printing there is no English edition.

Blanca G. Silvestrini and María D. Luque de Sánchez's *Historia de Puerto Rico: Trayectoria de un pueblo* (San Juan: Cultural Puertorriqueña, 1987) is another frequently used text in college courses on the island, as is Francisco A. Scarano's *Puerto Rico: Una Historia Contemporánea* (New York: McGraw-Hill, 2000).

Aida Negron de Montilla's *La Americanización de Puerto Rico y el Sistema de Instrucción Pública 1900–1930*, (San Juan: Universidad de Puerto Rico, 1977) is one of several classic texts that examine how the Puerto Rican school system was used to advance U.S. culture and political aims while suppressing traditional cultural expression among Puerto Rican school children, teachers, and families. Historian and educator Lidio Cruz Monclova's work covers some of the same ground, but also includes a focus on nineteenth century island history.

In *Biodervsidad de Puerto Rico* (San Juan: University of Puerto Rico, 2008), Rafael L. Joglar, a biology professor with dual appointments at the University of Kansas and the University of Puerto Rico, examines the natural history of the island through a series of photographs and essays. *Panorama historico forestal de Puerto Rico* by Carlos Dominguez Cristobal (San Juan: University of Puerto Rico, 2000) provides a comprehensive look at the island's most remote ecologies.

For a look at the history of women and feminism on the island, Spanish-speaking students may want to start with Yamila Azize Vargas' *La mujer en Puerto Rico* (Río Piedras: Editorial Huracán, 1987).

The United Nations Economic Commission for Latin America's report on Puerto Rico's economy, *Globalización y Desarrollo: Desafíos de Puerto Rico Frente al Siglo XXI*, was published in 2004.

For those looking to tackle primary document research from the early Spanish colonial period, among the 42 volumes that make up the *Colección de Documentos Inéditos Relativo al Descubrimiento* (*Collection of Unedited Documents Related to Discovery*) published in Spain between 1864 and 1884, are decrees, contracts, and correspondence between explorers in the Americas and officials in Castile, Aragon, and later Spain. It is believed that there is much un-mined source material in the collection, both for research and translation into English. Scholars generally agree that the new edition of *Cristóbal Colón: Textos y Documentos Completes* (*Christopher Columbus: The Complete Texts and Documents*) (Madrid: Alianza, 1992), edited by Consuelo Varela and Juan Gil, is far more complete and free of errors than previous comparable compilations.

ELECTRONIC SOURCES

Gobierno de Puerto Rico (the Puerto Rican government's Web site)

http://www.gobierno.pr/gprportal/inicio

CIA World Factbook, Puerto Rico

https://www.cia.gov/library/publications/the-world-factbook/geos/RQ.html

The Puerto Rico Encyclopedia (Web site of the Puerto Rican Humanities Foundation)

http://enciclopediapr.org/ing/

The Pew Hispanic Foundation

http://pewhispanic.org/

The Centro de Estudios Puertorriqueños at Hunter College, The City University of New York (Access to the Centro journal is available in PDF).

www.centropr.org

Teodoro Vidal Collection of Puerto Rican History at the Smithsonian Institute's National Museum of American History

http://americanhistory.si.edu/collections/group_detail.cfm?key=1253&gkey=78

El Nueva Dia, Puerto Rico's highest circulation daily, can be accessed at www.elnuevodia.com/

El Vocero, the newspaper with the second highest circulation on the island, can be accessed at www.elvocero.com

U.S. Census, Statistical Abstract, 2009, Section 29, Puerto Rico and Island Areas, www.census.gov/prod/2008pubs/09statab/outlying.pdf

More Census data can be found at Census Information Centers, http://www.census.gov/cic/

Archivo General de Puerto Rico, part of the Instituto de Cultura de Puerto Rico, http://www.icp.gobierno.pr/agp/index.htm

Museo de las Américas, Puerto Rico, http://www.prtc.net/~musame/

Centro de Estudios Avanzados de Puerto Rico y el Caribe, http://www.ceaprc.org/

The Puerto Rico Water Resources and Environmental Research Institute is another U.S. government-funded initiative, working with scholars from the University of Puerto Rico's College of Engineering and throughout the United States to share information on water resources, http://prwreri.uprm.edu/

National Institute for Latino Policy frequently hosts information on Puerto Ricans living on and off the island, http://www.latinopolicy.org/

There are a number of documentary films about Puerto Rico and the Puerto Rican Diaspora, among them, *The Borinquineers*, an award-winning exploration of Puerto Rico's 65th Infantry Regiment and Puerto Ricans in the military from

World War I to the present, with an emphasis on World War II and Korea. Directed by Noemi Figueroa Soulet and Raquel Ortiz, the film's web site is www.borinqueneers.com. *Yo Soy Boriqua, pa'que to lo sepas?* is a bilingual exploration of Puerto Rico's past and the history of the Puerto Rican Diaspora presented through vignettes hosted by actress, dancer, and co-director Rosie Perez. Co-directed by the prolific documentary filmmaker Liz Garbus, the film explores cultural and historic connections between the island and the Diaspora.

Index

Other Titles in the Greenwood Histories of the Modern Nations
Frank W. Thackeray and John E. Findling, Series Editors

The History of Afghanistan
Meredith L. Runion

The History of Argentina
Daniel K. Lewis

The History of Australia
Frank G. Clarke

The History of the Baltic States
Kevin O'Connor

The History of Brazil
Robert M. Levine

The History of Cambodia
Justin Corfield

The History of Canada
Scott W. See

The History of Central America
Thomas Pearcy

The History of Chile
John L. Rector

The History of China
David C. Wright

The History of Congo
Didier Gondola

The History of Cuba
Clifford L. Staten

The History of Egypt
Glenn E. Perry

The History of El Salvador
Christopher M. White

The History of Ethiopia
Saheed Adejumobi

The History of Finland
Jason Lavery

The History of France
W. Scott Haine

The History of Germany
Eleanor L. Turk

The History of Ghana
Roger S. Gocking

The History of Great Britain
Anne Baltz Rodrick

The History of Haiti
Steeve Coupeau

The History of Holland
Mark T. Hooker

The History of India
John McLeod

The History of Indonesia
Steven Drakeley

The History of Iran
Elton L. Daniel

The History of Iraq
Courtney Hunt

The History of Ireland
Daniel Webster Hollis III

The History of Israel
Arnold Blumberg

The History of Italy
Charles L. Killinger

The History of Japan, Second Edition
Louis G. Perez

The History of Korea
Djun Kil Kim

About the Author

LISA PIERCE FLORES began her journalism career at *El Nuevo Pais*, a daily newspaper in Caracas, Venezuela, and has since worked as a staff writer and editor at various newspapers, magazines, and trade and academic publishers. Her writing has appeared in *The Charlotte Observer*, *Inkwell*, *Stand Magazine*, and *The New York Times*. She teaches writing and journalism at Norwalk Community College. As editor of Greenwood/ABC-Clio's American Mosaic project [http://am.greenwood.com], she helped develop a suite of web sites and blogs exploring multiethnic America.